Praise for
Middle School Makeover
and Michelle Icard

"Icard, the creator of the middle school social skills courses Athena's Path and Hero's Pursuit, shares affirming, spot-on advice for guiding kids through the difficult middle school years, blending thoughtful practicality, and gentle humor. Icard recommends that parents serve as the calm 'assistant manager' to their children's growing brain, guiding them toward slower thinking and problem solving, and acting as empathetic coach rather than micromanager; she offers sample conversations to demonstrate what that might look like. Icard supports giving children greater independence, letting them take risks, and (monitored) use of social media, among many other helpful tips. Most importantly, Icard successfully positions herself as a knowledgeable, sympathetic peer— someone who knows that parents want to have a great relationship with their children during this period of rapid change." —*Publishers Weekly*

"*Middle School Makeover* is a great resource for anyone with a current or soon-to-be middle schooler in their life. With the voice of a friend, plenty of humor and lots of practical tips, Michelle Icard provides insight and answers to tween behaviors. *Middle School Makeover* also equips adults with useful 'to do' and 'to don't' tips for helping their middle schooler gain independence and confidence."

—Melisa Holmes, MD; founder, Girlology;
author of *Girlology: A Girl's Guide to Growing Up*

"Written with humor, empathy, and remarkable insight, *Middle School Makeover* feels less like a book and more like a conversation with friends over coffee. Parent-to-parent, Michelle Icard translates cutting-edge developmental research and professional terminology into plain language and practical advice for managing the many twists and turns of early adolescence. Most importantly, the book transforms the image of middle school as dreadful for kids and dreaded by parents into a stage of life that is unique, exciting, and full of potential. You will not look at your child, or perhaps even recall your own middle school years, in the same way again!"

—Beth A. Kotchick, PhD
associate professor,
Loyola University, Maryland

"Was middle school bad enough when you were going through it? Is facing middle school again through your child's experience giving you pause and anxiety? Worry no more. Michelle Icard has done an incredible job of offering parents not just the empathy they seek but the strategies they need to navigate their child's middle school year with wisdom, grace, and foresight. Icard so deftly blends storytelling, research, and guidance, you'll feel like you are having lunch with that smart, compassionate friend who never lets you feel defeated. *Middle School Makeover* will empower you to capably and calmly parent through the hard times and inspire you to celebrate through them, too."

—Rosie Molinary, author of *Beautiful You:*
A Daily Guide to Radical Self-Acceptance

"A makeover is desperately needed indeed. In twenty-five years of working with teenagers and their families, I've only had two people ask to volunteer to work with middle schoolers. In that same time, the stress that embraces parents is exactly what Michelle has described. *Middle School Makeover* is a book I will insist the families with whom I work and the students I teach have at their fingertips."

—Brian Foreman, EdD, youth ministry consultant and author
of *#Connect: Reaching Youth Across the Digital Divide and*
How to Be #SocialMediaParents. www.b4manconsutling.com

"*Middle School Makeover* is a masterpiece of how-tos for any parent dealing with the challenges of the middle school years. Parenting a middle schooler can be one of the most difficult times for parents to navigate. Michelle guides parents, using concrete solutions to real-life problems, faced by kids in their teen years. Michelle's practical advice and humorous writing style make for an easy read for busy parents on-the-go."

—Seanna Crosbie, LCSW clinical therapist and director, Child Guidance Center, Texas

"Every middle school parent, teacher, and child would benefit greatly from this makeover. With clear writing, warmth, and humor, Icard offers straightforward paths through some of the bumpier aspects of the dark, scary place known as Middle School. She weaves personal anecdotes together with research and expert insights to give parents and educators all the tools they will need to navigate this phase with their child. By addressing not just the needs of the middle schooler but the middle school parent as well, she reveals herself to be the perfect ally during this sometimes tumultuous phase. But Icard's greatest gift and the book's primary accomplishment is how it subtly shifts our expectations of middle school. By the end, every reader will feel that this is not a phase to be feared, but celebrated and enjoyed. We highly recommend to anyone who lives or works with middle schoolers."

—Erin Dymowski and Ellen Williams,
Sisterhood of the Sensible Moms
www.sisterhoodofthesensiblemoms.com

"*Middle School Makeover* is a must read for anyone who has or works with middle students. Michelle brings understanding, compassion and wisdom to caring for this much misunderstood group of young people. I encourage every middle school parent to pick up this book, your middle schooler will be so glad you did!"

—Vicki Abadesco! co-founder, Soul Shoppe
author of *Free to Be: Creating a Safe,
Fun & Bully-Free World*

"Michelle's book is a terrific blend of solid research, innovative ideas, and good old-fashioned experience with adolescents. There are a lot of books full of buzz words and generic advice, but Michelle's book drills down into specifics: what to say, how to say it, how not to say it, and the facial expression to show while saying it. The book hits on many of those tough social situations that leave adults struggling for words when it comes to advising their children. In my job as a school counselor, I reach for her material when trying to guide a middle school student (or parent of a middle-schooler) through a very trying and very real situation."

—Wes Calbreath, MEd Middle School Counselor
at Charlotte-Mecklenburg School System

MIDDLE SCHOOL
MAKEOVER

MIDDLE
SCHOOL
MAKEOVER

Improving the Way You and Your Child
Experience the Middle School Years

MICHELLE ICARD

bibliomotion
books + media

First published by Bibliomotion, Inc.
39 Harvard Street
Brookline, MA 02445
Tel: 617-934-2427
www.bibliomotion.com

Printed in the United States of America

Library of Congress Cataloging-in-Publication Data

Icard, Michelle.
    Middle school makeover : improving the way you and your child experience the middle school years / Michelle Icard.
        pages cm
    Summary: "Middle School Makeover is a guide for parents and educators to help tweens navigate their middle school years"— Provided by publisher.
    ISBN 978-1-937134-97-6 (paperback) — ISBN 978-1-937134-98-3 (ebook) — ISBN 978-1-937134-99-0 (enhanced ebook)
    1. Middle school students.   2. Middle school students—Social conditions.
3. Middle school students—Psychology.   4. Child development.   5. Adolescence.
6. Parenting.   I. Title.
    HQ796.I228 2014
    373.236—dc23
                        2013049433

To my favorite middle schoolers, Ella and Declan. I look forward to seeing you as the first brother–sister duo on Saturday Night Live. *Thank you for keeping Dad and me (your biggest fans) laughing. I love you so much my heart might burst.*

—Mom

Contents

Foreword

Middle school looms for some parents the way the wedding night looms—or loomed—for many a generation: Exciting!

Terrifying.

And nothing will ever be the same again.

Actually, all that is true—for you and for your kids. The good news is that no matter how surprising and tumultuous, you will all get through it, and you will probably be very happy to see your kids growing more independent each year. The other good news (Ha ha—I bet you were expecting bad news, right?) is that you have Michelle Icard with you on this journey.

I met Michelle when were we both on a panel with the title of, "What You Need to Know as Parents" —or something like that. I spoke first and weighed in on how our kids are smarter and more competent than our scaredy-cat society tells us they are. From perverts to predators to the perils of a non-organic grape, the dangers have all been overblown, and the upshot is: helicopter parenting.

That was everything the audience needed to know, I figured. Then Michelle took the mic and started explaining what happens to kids—physically, socially, emotionally and even technologically—when they reach the middle school years.

I rummaged in my purse for paper and pen and started taking notes.

Insight! So much insight! Michelle has studied middle-schoolers the way Madame Curie studied radium. (Except the middle-schoolers have not killed Michelle.) (Yet.) She's not an alarmist. She's just very smart, with the compassion and tips borne of helping a whole lot of kids and parents in the real world. What she knows could fill a book!

In fact, it did. You're holding it.

So what are you waiting for? Read it! You'll be glad you did.

—Lenore Skenazy
founder of the book,
blog and movement *Free-Range Kids*

Introduction

How and Why This Book Works

Middle school has never been easy. For that matter, neither has being a parent. Put them together and…"Hey, you got your parenting into my middle school years!" meets "You got your middle school years into my parenting!" and…eureka! Like the old Reese's Peanut Butter Cups ad, what seems like a calamity ends up being a great combination. By the time you finish this book, you'll see how parents and middle schoolers don't inevitably have to clash and you'll learn ways you and your child can work together to make these next few years easier and more enjoyable.

You may feel, now that your kid is in—or heading to—middle school, that you can finally loosen up your parenting style. Or, you may think it's time to tighten the screws. In fact, the key to having a happier middle school experience for you and your child has nothing to do with you backing off *or* clamping down. The key is doing something different.

> Middle school is a parenting game changer, and you'll be surprised how a few simple changes will make your life and your child's much more pleasant through the tricky middle school years.

WHY THIS BOOK?

Chances are, you've picked up this book because you have a child in, or heading to, middle school. That, or you're a relative of mine. Either way, thank you. If you're the former, I know two things for sure: you've got questions and you're in a hurry.

I can relate to how hectic life is at this stage. I know I'm supposed to "live in the moment," "breathe," and "be present." I've read the bumper stickers. Theoretically, I'm on board. But as a busy mom who also runs my own business, sometimes what makes me feel best is crossing stuff off my list so I can get to the part of my day where I sit myself down on the couch and watch *Top Chef*.

The reason I share that with you is because I want you to know that this book is designed to accommodate your lifestyle. It's written at a fast pace and in an easy-to-read style, with practical solutions to the most common problems I see families of middle schoolers face.

RESEARCH AND EXPERIENCE

So that your middle school makeover will be quick and pain-less, I have read the research, analyzed it for you, and digested the information into easy action and speech you can integrate into your life. I give you suggestions for what to say and when to say it, so that dealing with middle school social turmoil can be as painless as possible.

> My advice is based on what the latest science tells us about adolescents, as well as my own experience working with middle schoolers and their parents for the past decade.

Ten years ago, I launched a program called Athena's Path to help girls learn skills for navigating the turbulent middle school social scene. Shortly after, I developed a brother program, Hero's Pursuit, to help boys in the same way. Since then, my curriculum has been implemented in six states as a class during the school day. I've trained hundreds of teachers and countless parents on how to help kids survive and thrive in middle school. My website, MichelleintheMiddle.com, gives parents a place where they can go for advice and relief from the middle school drama in their lives. Plus, I've got middle schoolers of my own at home. I've been living and breathing all things middle school for the past decade, during which time I've developed strong beliefs about this critical period in kids' lives.

I believe:

- The middle school years can and should be fun for kids and parents.
- Kids in middle school need and deserve more freedom to explore who they are outside of their parents.
- Parents can take their middle schooler's accomplishments and failures seriously without taking them personally.
- Raising middle schoolers is very different from raising elementary schoolers, and requires parents to change the way they relate to their kids.
- The social world of middle school is incredibly important to a child's development and should be treated with respect.

WHAT I LOVE ABOUT MIDDLE SCHOOLERS

It's true, middle schoolers do a lot of things that make you go, "Hmmm…" or in some cases, *"What?!"* They can be baffling and frustrating, but I prefer to see them as inspirational and impressive. A quick study of young adult novels, the characters in them and our kids' reactions to them, will show us there is no creature more empathetic toward those who suffer social injustice, more compelled by optimism and faith in humankind, or more aspirational in her beliefs than a middle schooler.

> Little kids believe in fantasy magic like Santa, fairies, and dragons. Middle schoolers believe in real-world magic like justice, hope, and infinite possibility.

THE MIDDLE SCHOOL SOCIAL WORLD IS IMPORTANT

As the parent of a child in, or transitioning to, middle school you are probably recalling your own adolescent memories more frequently these days. Dropping off at preschool was heart-wrenching, but something about sending your child through those big middle school doors among the masses of suddenly supersized kids can fill your veins with the icy fear of mean girls, pubescent boys, rumors, parties, cliques, and bad hair days as if you were in middle school all over again. I can almost smell the Noxema now...

At no time is our sense of parental security more rocked than during the middle school years. Why is it so? Your child, although progressing happily with his social, emotional, physical, and intellectual development to this point, upon entering middle school begins to embark on a major construction project to build the three things he needs to be an adult: a grown-up body, a mature brain, and a unique identity. This is his primary job in middle school—and it's an awesome task—all the while trying to keep up good grades and participate in extracurricular activities.

This construction project will get very sloppy. The middle school years are filled with impulsive mistakes, overflowing emotions, irrational misunderstandings, and even new and shocking smells.

> You thought diaper changes were rough? Wait until you experience the aroma of middle school. Brace yourself.

Complicating the inherent difficulties of building a body, brain, and identity is the significant fact that this particular construction project is being built on unsteady ground. Imagine constructing a house on the beach at low tide. Shifting sands and changing tides are naturally going to rock the foundation. If your child's "house" is his new body, brain, and identity project, then the unstable "beach" below him is the middle school social scene.

Nothing takes up more brain space for your child than figuring out how to maintain his balance in the new social order while also figuring out what to do with gangly legs, impulsive thoughts, and self-doubt.

Your child's success in the middle school years, and well into adulthood, relies on his ability to successfully navigate his social scene so that the bumpy terrain doesn't throw his psychological and emotional development too far off kilter. Creating a strong foundation in the social world will make the construction project go much more smoothly because the challenges of the social world routinely cause kids to second-guess themselves. You see this when your daughter shuts down after being teased for developing too early or too late (body doubt), when your son confesses he didn't want to take "that dare" but he didn't know how to say no without looking scared (brain doubt), or when your typically polite daughter gets called to the principal's office for bullying (identity doubt).

The good news is that you can help your child learn how to

respond to his changing social scene in a way that builds his confidence. Parenting a middle schooler is very different from parenting an elementary schooler, and it's not entirely intuitive. Most of all, this requires a major paradigm shift from fixing things for your child to teaching your child how to fix things himself. Middle school is the exact right time to do this, so your child can build the critical thinking, problem solving, and self-reliance skills he needs to be a success.

I cannot stress enough, as parents we must take the middle school social scene seriously. It's easy, and often more comfortable, to put up walls, ignore trends, and shy away from what's happening on the bus, in the hallway, in the cafeteria, and at friends' houses. It would be easier to focus on grades and curfew than on crushes, dares, kissing, and drinking. Parenting a middle schooler is not for the faint of heart.

There are so many easy ways you can make the middle school years better for your child and you, too. By the time you finish reading this book you will know:

- How the key tasks of body, brain, and identity development will affect your middle schooler and why your parenting approach must adapt to address these changes.
- What really happens in middle school today and how it differs from when we were there.
- How to teach your child to independently and creatively solve her own problems.
- The best way to get your child to honestly open up to you about middle school life.
- Exactly what to say and do when your child comes to you with the common middle school social dilemmas kids face.
- How to practice taking care of yourself during this time, too.

Ready? Grab your backpack. We're headed back to middle school.

PART 1

The Foundation for Parenting Middle Schoolers

HOW THIS BOOK WORKS

In the next five chapters, I'll give you a simple foundation of theories you'll need to understand and distill the advice I dispense in the second half of the book, where I'll get very practical and specific about scenarios that are probably happening at your home and what you can do and say to manage them. You may be tempted, in your search for answers, to flip right to the second half of the book and find the solution to your problems, but I encourage you to read through the first section to help you commit to the new solutions I'll introduce. Otherwise, they may not make sense. Then, keep this book handy, tucked into your car door or perched on your nightstand, so that when a situation arises, you can flip and find the help you need.

"WHAT YOU TALKIN' 'BOUT, WILLIS?"

One more important instruction for how to use this book is to remember *with empathy* what it was like when you were young. My writing is heavily peppered with references to '70s and '80s pop culture, which informed my coming of age and probably yours, too. Mostly, this is because I think they're funny and I can't help myself. But they also serve a higher purpose, reminding us that we can't overlook the important influence of pop culture on our kids' social development. What better way to see this than through a nostalgic lens that brings into focus the effects of pop culture on our own development. You feel me? No? Kiss my grits.

Now let's begin, as any decent makeover should, with a good foundation.

1

What's a Middle School Makeover?

Visit any elementary school near the end of the academic year, and you'll hear parents lamenting the transition to middle school.

"I'm so nervous for her!"
"We just don't know what to expect."
"I hated middle school."
"Poor thing, he's got such an awkward couple of years ahead."
"I'm dreading the bad attitude!"
"I'm dreading the bad influences!"
"I'm dreading it all."
And so on.

Middle school gets a bad rap. Even the name implies that it's a no-man's-land, stuck in the middle between cute elementary school and important high school. Historically, this has been the case. You probably remember going to junior high, not middle school. In the mid-1960s middle schools slowly began replacing junior high schools as part of an effort to distinguish between a model of kids attending "little high school" and a new concept where the unique developmental needs of kids ages eleven to fourteen could be addressed right along with their academic needs.[1] Whether or not developmental needs are truly addressed in today's middle schools is questionable. Instead, many parents see middle school as a tumultuous, hormone-driven, attitude-filled, peer pressure and rebellion–ruled subsociety where every kid must serve time before gaining entrance to the happy world of high school.

In part, that's because it's the socially acceptable thing to think. We aren't *supposed* to like the fact that our daughters are becoming interested in boys, that our sons are cutting up in class to make girls laugh, that makeup and deodorant and feminine hygiene products and cell phones and expensive sneakers are littering already too-messy rooms. We feel we're supposed to complain about our kids making their own decisions, and making a mess while they do it, because that's what parents of kids this age talk about. We gripe to each other to form a common bond over how awful it all is, and we joke about needing wine therapy and about how much we dread the dating and driving and drinking soon to follow. We pretend misery loves company when what it really craves is a new perspective.

It's time for a middle school makeover.

I know that times have changed since we were in school, and our kids face more challenging situations than we ever imagined. But, we've created a self-fulfilling prophecy in which, for many kids and parents, middle school really does stink, in part because we fully expect that it should. Did you know that in many other cultures there is no such saying as the terrible twos?[2] In countries like ours, where we have a high regard for all individuals, we expect toddlers to integrate into our family systems just like every other member of the family. To an exploratory two-year-old, that means he must share, adjust to adult schedules, and comply with adult norms. Cue crying and pounding of fists. In other countries, parents expect older family members to forgo their own needs so that a toddler's unique needs and desires may be tended to. The result is, you guessed it, happy and compliant two-year-olds, and that leads to happy parents.

Why am I even mentioning two-year-olds when this is a book about middle school? Because two-year-olds and twelve-year-olds have a lot more in common than you might think. Like a toddler, your middle schooler is learning how to operate a new body, identity, emotions, desires, and intellectual thoughts. Talking about this like it's a big, ugly process and worrying about how messy it might become, or ordering him to learn how to control himself to fit into your family's structure, is counterproductive. (Cue crying and pounding of fists.)

The middle school makeover is about improving the way we think about the middle school years. What if, instead of dreading middle school, we got excited about it? There is a lot of magic that happens during the middle school years and it has the potential to be one of the best times of your parenting life...if you can see middle school through a new lens.

One of the first steps in doing that is getting rid of your own middle school baggage. We often send our kids into middle school carrying more than that already-too-heavy book bag. In addition to forty pounds of books, binders, and pens, they might be burdened by expectations or worries built on our own memories of bullies, popularity, social pressure, exclusion, growing up too fast...you name it.

I surveyed one hundred parents of kids in third, fourth, and fifth grades about their expectations for parenting middle schoolers.

25 percent said they had a definitively bad experience in middle school
30 percent had a definitively good experience in middle school
45 percent had some good experiences and some bad experiences

Of the 25 percent who had a definitively bad experience, half could not identify *one thing* to look forward to about their kid going to middle school. Sample comments from these parents were:

"Nothing. Most other parents identify this time as one you have to 'survive.' I rarely hear positive things about it."

"Excited about middle school? Nope, nothing, I am not looking
forward to the next three years AT ALL..."
"Nothing, I'm scared for him."
"To be completely honest, not much! They are crummy years!"
"Nothing. Wish we could skip it altogether."
"Mostly, I dread middle school."

I understand. It's been thirty years since I walked the halls of seventh grade (ouch), yet I still have a vivid recollection of the people
and events that characterized these short but important two years
of my life. Maybe, like me, you can recall the stuff that happened
in middle school—embarrassing moments, friendship betrayals, first
kisses—with high-definition clarity. It was the first time in your life,
after all, that you dabbled in total independence from your parents,
concentrating your mixed feelings of excitement, doubt, guilt, and
pride as you tried to figure out who you were in this world.

I encourage you, as you read this book, to do two things.

**Think back on your middle school experience and distill it
from your child's.** One way to do this is to watch your middle
school moments like a movie with some detachment and, if you've
cast yourself in a victim role, take yourself out of it. Give your
younger self some grace toward the mistakes you made. Harder still,
give those kids who mistreated you not one more second thought.
That was a reflection of their bad decision making, not yours.

Reframe the way you think about middle school in general.
When you talk about middle school, use words like "opportunity"
and "exciting." Before long, you'll have created a self-fulfilling
prophesy of the nicest kind.

MY STORY

To help you get to know me a little better, and as an example of exorcising middle school baggage, I'd like to share with you my middle school story.

In fifth grade, I attended Brooks Elementary School in Medford, Massachusetts. This was the third of four elementary schools I would attend. How to describe Brooks Elementary... did you ever see Michelle Pfeiffer in *Dangerous Minds*? Not that bad. Those kids were hard-core criminals! Let's say about one-tenth that bad. Did you ever see *Meatballs*? About twice that bad. Brooks had a staff that could not have cared less and an out-of-control student body comprised overwhelmingly of dim-witted pranksters and soon-to-be juvenile delinquents.

Needless to say, the academics at Brooks were far from rigorous. I remember my fifth-grade teacher explaining her grading system to us: "If you turn it in on time, it's an 'A.' A day late, it's a 'B.' After that, a 'C.'" And so on. My parents grew alarmed. This would not do. One weekend they told me they were taking me to a private school for admissions testing. If I could get in, they would figure out a way to pay.

Easier said than done. The cost was about $13,000 per year back in 1983, the equivalent of about $30,000 today, although current tuition is $39,000 per year without boarding. The point is, it was very expensive.

I did get in, and that must have been a mixed blessing to my parents. We were not wealthy and paying tuition meant taking out loans, but my parents, thankfully, were committed to giving me the best possible education.

My new school, Buckingham, Browne & Nichols, (BB&N for short) was exactly what it sounds like: a beautiful, well-endowed, and exclusive New England prep school with a student body comprised of the wealthy children of Boston's elite (plus a few kids like me thrown in for diversity). As the start of school drew closer, I became increasingly nervous about becoming a private school kid. Would I fit in? Would I make friends? Would I have the right clothes?

Of course I wouldn't have the right clothes! I had "public school clothes." I asked my parents if I could get some fancy clothes to start my fancy school, but their money was all tied up in tuition. I would have to go as I was.

Nuh-uh. "Going as I was" was entirely unacceptable. Did Willis and Arnold *"go as they were"* to Digby Prep when Mr. Drummond tried to enroll them? No! They put on sweater vests and wool slacks and marched to the beat of their own drum by fitting in. Did Jo Polniaczek *"go as she was"* to Eastland School with Mrs. Garrett? No! Jo may have pulled her necktie askew, but she still wore the uniform and looked pretty much like every other girl there. If TV taught me anything about poor kids straddling the economic divide, it was that a large dose of sassy attitude and the right "uniform" were essential to fitting in.

(It occurs to me now that my primary education on how poor kids behaved around rich people came entirely from '80s television sitcoms. Clearly, this was a major part of my problem.)

Because my new school did not require us to wear uniforms like my sitcom role models, I needed to get creative about my wardrobe. I did what any self-respecting tween would do (any who couldn't actually sew like Molly Ringwald in *Pretty in Pink*): I called my grandmother. She offered to buy me *one* new outfit to start my new school. I needed only to be sure it was killer.

The year was 1983. You may recall a new TV show had recently aired called *Silver Spoons*, in which Ricky Schroder played a rich teen living in a mansion with a working train to transport him from room to room, among other cool things.

Ricky was the quintessential rich kid and I *knew* I needed to dress like him to make a good impression at my new school.

My attempt to look like a successful and
wealthy private school kid. Nailed it!

This is my sixth-grade class picture. I chose the most corporate outfit I could find for an eleven-year-old girl. That's right, I was a girl back then. Don't let the haircut fool you. If I could have afforded a briefcase, I would have bought that, too.

DAY ONE OF SIXTH GRADE

Wearing my eggplant dress slacks, puffy-sleeved dress shirt, matching eggplant rayon bow tie, and sporting a back-porch haircut, I walked into my new classroom. And someone laughed. Someone looked directly at me and laughed. I felt like *everyone* laughed, but it was probably just one or two kids. Still, that was all it took for me to slink to the back of the room and avoid talking to anyone else for the rest of the day.

Dr. Charisse Nixon, a professor of developmental psychology

at Penn State, has done some fascinating work around the concept of learned helplessness among adolescents. Her YouTube video on learned helplessness, posted as part of The Ophelia Project, depicts a startling activity Dr. Nixon does with her college classes, in which she renders one half of the class academically helpless in about two minutes flat, using nothing but a word jumble.[3] Dr. Nixon explains that the same thing happens to kids socially. One or two social failures can lead to a total meltdown of confidence, after which kids quickly stop trying, in effect becoming socially helpless.

So on day one of sixth grade, two minutes into my new school, I was already socially helpless. My dreams of finding a Blair, Tootie, or Natalie to hang out with were dashed; I resigned myself to being a loser. This was not what I signed up for.

While I fantasized about riding from class to class on a miniature train in my corporate raider attire, campaigning for and winning the coveted role of sixth-grade class president, attending mixers with my classmates, and talking about "rich stuff" over heaping bowls of Doritos and M&Ms, it just wasn't going to turn out that way.

Thus began my long career as an introvert. In just one day, I cast myself as the shy girl, a role that I played well for many years.

On the upside, later that sixth-grade year, I made one friend. She was the world to me. I'll call her Hannah. We were best friends and did nearly everything together that school year. On Wednesdays, our school ended at one o'clock in the afternoon. Perfect, because *Days of Our Lives* started at one. We would run from school, through Harvard Square to her house and down her basement steps, where we would indulge in the grown-up fantasies of middle-aged women. Hannah's neighborhood was filled with the beautiful homes of Harvard professors and local celebrities (Julia Child lived right behind her), and I don't think there was a TV in the living portion of the home. This meant her basement was our secret getaway, where we could watch our shows and eat copious amounts of Ritz Crackers. I was so, so happy there.

ALL OF SEVENTH GRADE

BB&N was divided into a lower, middle, and upper school campus. In seventh grade, our class bumped up to the middle school campus and we received an influx of new students. One of them I'll call Rachel. We hit it off instantly. Hannah, Rachel, and I were three peas in a pod. Uh-oh. You know what happens with a group of three girls.

So it was weird when I would call one of them to suggest we all get together, but they were already hanging out. This happened a few times, but I was slow to catch on. Rachel and I carpooled, but she stopped speaking to me in the car. I was getting a severely cold shoulder that left me stranded in middle school feeling very alone. I began noticing every eye roll, every insult, every private joke that kept me on the outs. Walking down the hall, I kept my eyes on the floor for fear of anyone noticing me and making fun.

Guess jeans were the fashion standard that year. Still desperate to fit in but unable to afford the expensive clothes worn by the popular girls, I bought a pair of Jet jeans. Please don't confuse these with the JET jeans worn by celebrities like Kim Kardashian these days. My Jets were decidedly off-brand. I thought they were cool enough. Jet sort of sounded like Guess...I guess.

I was a timid Jet jean girl in a too-cool Guess jean world. And the eighth-grade girls noticed. There was one eighth grader at my school who dressed like Madonna. I mean a full-on, 1985, "Like a Virgin" Madonna. She was terrifying. On the bus to and from sports she would pull down her window and suck on a lollipop seductively whenever a man pulled up next to us at a stoplight. I did not know *what* to make of her.

Naturally, she and her friends noticed my Jet jeans. More importantly, they noticed the way I was always alone and afraid to make eye contact. That started many lonely months of being teased openly and relentlessly about my clothes. I hated school. I got stomachaches and wanted to stay home. One day on the bus, I sat alone in the front row behind the driver, while Madonna and her friends pelted food at the back of my head. I remember thinking if I just stayed quiet and didn't look at them, they would stop.

The sad irony is that my parents were shelling out thousands of dollars they didn't actually have to give me an extraordinary education, but all I could focus on was becoming invisible. I never engaged in class. I never raised my hand. I was so afraid of people seeing me, and not liking what they saw, that I tried to disappear.

This is how middle school passed for me, like a far too slow and lonely walk through thick mud. But then came high school.

FINALLY, A LITTLE DRAMA! (THE GOOD KIND)

I spent my final four years at BB&N on the upper school campus, and it was there that two important things happened to me.

In ninth grade, I tried out for the musical. How does a girl afraid of being seen in middle school decide one year later to put herself on stage? At the time it wasn't obvious to me, but now I see that being on stage gave me a compelling opportunity to be someone else for a change. I was one of four freshmen to be cast in the musical, and at that point my life changed. People noticed me, and I *liked* it. I started making eye contact with kids in the hall, wondering with hope, "Do they recognize me? Have they heard me sing?"

The other thing that happened was that I changed physically. My previously buck teeth, after four miserable years of braces and headgear, were finally straight. This put an end to one of my father's favorite jokes about me being able to eat corn through a chain link fence. Hysterical! Also, I traded in my glasses for contacts and started devoting some serious time to "styling" my hair.

My beauty regimen, consisting of these essential products, became very important to me:

- Baby oil (to be applied while lying out on a towel on my driveway)
- Blue eyeliner
- Frosted pink lipstick
- Brown blush
- Aerosol hairspray

Funny what a little bit of confidence and $10 at CVS will get you: noticed by guys, that's what. I was by no stretch popular and I'm not sure my classmates thought I was pretty. Cute, maybe? But you have no idea how insurmountable "cute" felt to that girl in the sixth-grade class picture. If you haven't already guessed, I'll tell you that finally being found attractive, even just attractive *enough*, made me long for further acceptance from my peers. I had my toe in the door and I wanted more. Being rendered a misfit in middle school had a solid effect on my high school days, too.

> Our experience in middle school sets the foundation for what we believe about ourselves in high school and beyond.

I believed my value came from the way I looked. But although my exterior changed and I finally found a space where I belonged, my inner misfit was still controlling my every move. I took too many risks in search of praise. I put too much emphasis on my outward appearance. I was not strong enough to stick up for anyone in need. I was utterly filled with doubt.

In fact, the results of my middle school experience extended long past high school. I spent too much energy putting up walls so that people wouldn't see the real me. My biggest fear was being vulnerable. Even as an adult, I have been reluctant to expose too much of myself, even the parts of myself I like, because to expose my favorite qualities and then be rejected? That would be unbearable.

WHY IS MIDDLE SCHOOL SO STICKY?

Perhaps you can relate to my story and to that feeling of being the awkward one. Can you still remember the name of that girl in middle school who made you feel not good enough? Or how it felt to be picked last in gym class? Can you also recall the name of a kid in middle school who went out of his way to make you feel good about yourself? Amazing how after all these years (twenty-five, thirty, thirty-five years?) those memories come back so quickly.

When I ask adults, "If you could magically be transported through time to a week in middle school, would you do it?" almost all of them give a variation on, "No way in hell." "Not for a million dollars," I've been told many times. Isn't that bizarre? Why is it that the stuff that happens to us in middle school can stay so raw, for so long? What is it about middle school that makes it "stick"?

The short answer is that middle school is when you begin the important job of developing an identity. For the first time in your life, you begin asking the profound question, "Who am I apart from my parents?" Every rude comment, eye roll, heavy sigh, giggle, smile, and high five from your peers helps to form the answer that embeds itself into your developing brain.

Our middle school makeover begins with shedding any negative thoughts you still carry around from your own experience and preparing to support your child's independent experience, by being enthusiastic and hopeful about this new phase of your kid's life.

2

Middle School Brains Are Different

Like many of you, my middle school–aged children have social media accounts. I know social media frightens some parents, but in general I support social media use among tweens and teens. I think it's a great arena for creativity, community, and communication. But every yin must have its yang, and social media also offers opportunities for the tween brain to showcase its shortcomings.

Let's dive right into the deep end, shall we?

Recently, I was scrolling through Instagram and I saw the most upsetting image I've seen in a long time. Picture this: two seventh-grade boys facing the camera and leaning up against a big rock outside school. Also facing the camera, but leaning up against the boys, were two seventh-grade girls. One of the girls was covering her face as though she were embarrassed. The other was looking down at the ground. Both boys were grinning ear to ear; both girls were not. The boys had their arms reaching around the girls from behind, and their hands cupping the girls' breasts. The caption read, "Gettin' sexual." I did not know any of the kids in the picture, but I did know the boy who posted it, a mannerly—if girl-crazy—boy from our neighborhood pool.

The caption and the boys' poses were both goofy and gross, but the upsetting part was the girls' expressions. They seemed humiliated. In the same moment I wished that their parents both would and would not see the picture.

What is it that happens between the end of elementary school and the beginning of middle school that causes kids to suddenly behave with so little rational thought and so much... what's the word I'm looking for? Oh yes, stupidity.

I don't think the boys in that picture were being malicious. I think they had a flash of momentary idiocy that led to (1) mistreating those girls, (2) taking a picture of it, and (3) posting that picture to a public forum. Usually, kids don't think these things through, and if they do, their response might by something like, "Big deal. Who's gonna see it anyway?" So I offer this timely yet digressive reminder: I'm writing about my neighbor's Instagram post in a book. You never know where *your* post will end up.

Remember the not-so-smart things you, or the kids you went to school with, did in middle school? I knew kids who "borrowed" their parents' cars to go around the block, who spent more than "Seven Minutes" in a closet with someone they didn't like, who cheated on tests, and who obsessively prank called innocent sleepers in the middle of the night. (Okay, that last one might have been me.) Naturally, parents want to blame someone or something when their kids go off the rails. We can't, however, attribute what happens to kids in middle school solely to bad parenting, lack of after-school activities, too many after-school activities, bad genes, goofy peers, a media-obsessed culture, or the dark side of social media. Adolescent missteps, after all, transcend all social classes, family types, cultures, and other personal circumstances. They also transcend time. With each new generation, kids still take the same risks, proving again and again how biologically rooted this phenomenon is among tweens and teens.

As the novelist Douglas Coupland wrote, "Blame is just the lazy person's way of making sense of chaos." So rather than look for outside forces to blame for the crazy stuff kids start doing in middle school, we really just need to understand what's happening inside their brains, the real driving force behind all their actions.

Do any of the following sound familiar?

Your kid:

- Acts like a very bad lawyer, coming to a conclusion first, then trying to cram a bunch of absurd evidence together to support her theory
- Begins to care a great deal what her peers are doing, wearing, saying, listening to, and watching
- Decides that, across the board, you don't know very much
- Cries easily over small things
- Accuses you of being mad, often
- Does idiotic things when you *know* he knows better!
- Withdraws from family time
- Forgets things: homework, where he put his shoes, what you said, etc.

Congratulations. You've got a middle schooler. When compiled in list form, these behaviors sound hideous and would cause any parent to check his kid's return policy. But when you understand what's happening to the middle schooler's brain, you can see the purpose behind the behaviors and perhaps even have some gratitude for this tricky time in your kid's social development.

To begin, you'll need a crash course in what's happening inside your kid's noggin.

Brain development is one of my favorite topics. The differences between adult and adolescent brains have been studied only since the early 1990s, so the research is still considered groundbreaking. It's amazing what's going on in the middle schooler's mind.

YOUR MIDDLE SCHOOL-AGED TODDLER

Your kid's brain is only about halfway developed during the middle school years. In fact, a girl's brain reaches full biological maturity at age twenty-two, a boy's brain at age twenty-eight. Do the math and you'll see that girls reach their development half-life at age eleven and boys, not until age fourteen.[1] At the start of middle school, major brain changes begin happening, and this can generate some wacky behavior in both genders. To ease the anxiety this can cause both parent and child, it helps if you can reframe the way you think about weird middle school behavior. When your kid started to toddle, it was scary at times, like when she would tumble onto concrete or bang her head on a corner, but...it was also exciting. You cheered her on through every tumble because that is how she learned to be bigger, stronger, and more self-reliant. You didn't want to carry her on your hip forever.

With brain development, the tumbles aren't as easy to spot, or as adorable. But, if you can adopt the same attitude toward learning to use an adult brain that you did toward learning to walk, it's easier to have empathy and be supportive through this unsteady time. When your kid stumbles, as he inevitably must in order to learn to use his developing brain properly, it's fine to correct him. Just try to also maintain sympathy for how weak his decision making, impulse control, and critical thinking skills are at this stage. Regardless of how smart, thoughtful, and respectful your child may be...the part of the brain responsible for these skills just isn't fully developed yet. You wouldn't yell at a toddler for having weak leg muscles and falling down. But you might restrict his access to dangerous steps. Wouldn't it be nice if you could "tween-proof" your home with bumper pads on every sharp corner? But the kinds of tumbles your tween will take are more likely to bruise an ego (his *or* yours) than a leg.

Parenting through the middle school years is fraught with dichotomies, including this: you want your kid to learn from you and benefit from your hard-earned wisdom, while at the same time you want your child to become an independent and critical thinker. The key to balancing these desires is to become a good "assistant manager."

BECOMING A GOOD ASSISTANT MANAGER

The front of the brain is called the prefrontal cortex and it's the area of the brain responsible for such complex jobs as critical thinking, impulse control, and moderating social behavior. Pause for a moment and ask yourself, "Do I know anyone who isn't particularly good at critical thinking, impulse control, and moderating social behavior?" Chances are, someone between the ages of ten and eighteen popped into your head. There are many adults, of course, who lack these skills. Those I know suffered from some developmental trauma that stunted their brain development during adolescence, and this part of their brain seems to have never fully developed.

The prefrontal cortex is the part of the brain that is responsible for high-level judgment and analysis. You might call the prefrontal cortex the manager of your brain. I have some potentially upsetting information to report. For the next seven to ten years, your kid's manager is going on a big, fat lunch break. That part of her brain is under construction and will not be functioning at full capacity until her early twenties.

There's good reason for that manager to be taking such a long break. I'll cover *why* this happens in the next chapter, but for now, it's important that you and your middle schooler both understand that the part of the brain used to make careful, thoughtful, and informed decisions isn't working at its best right now. Explain to your child that the manager of her brain is on break and that she's going to need an assistant manager to sub in for a while. Who's that? I'll give you a hint. That person is currently reading this book.

Because impulse control is not yet hardwired into your child's changing brain, you must sometimes step in to slow down his thinking process. The secret to doing this is much like the secret to being a good leader in other aspects of your life. Take a moment and ask yourself, "Who are the best bosses I've worked for or seen in action?" Did they:

- Give you consistent feedback?
- Set clear expectations?
- Communicate clearly when you did something well?
- Give you constructive criticism without becoming emotional?
- Respect your personal life?
- Encourage you to take risks to grow?
- Provide you with opportunities to try new things?
- Show a willingness to learn from you?
- Have fun at work and enjoy their role?

As you begin to notice and reflect on the qualities of a good boss, begin applying those principles to your relationship with your middle schooler. In the same way, you can begin to identify the qualities of a bad boss and begin striking those from your parenting style. My personal bad boss pet peeve is being micromanaged.

DON'T BE A MICROMANAGER

Being micromanaged does not feel good. To be an effective assistant manager to your kid through adolescence, you need to teach him to think critically, *not* do it for him.

The prefrontal cortex may not be fully developed and your

child's brain manager may be on lunch break, but that doesn't mean you need to step in with 100 percent of the decision making for your tween. It's important that your child practice critical thinking and decision making a lot during the middle school years. If not, his developing brain will think these aren't important skills and they won't be hardwired into his brain. That's a scary thought. By letting your child practice these skills, you actually help set them into your kid's forming brain like handprints in concrete, so that they become hardened into place later in life. Miss this opportunity to put these skills into practice, and your child's brain will have developed to maturity in his twenties without them.

If you have ever been micromanaged by a boss, partner, parent, or even a friend, I'll bet it didn't inspire you to perform your best or feel very proud of your accomplishments in that situation. Multiply that feeling exponentially to imagine how crushing micromanagement can feel in the brain of a tween trying to assert some much-needed independence in the world. Although your child needs you to help manage her decision making during the tween and teen years, like any good boss, you will get better results if you guide rather than control your child's choices.

I was raised by a stepfather who applied orderly, logical systems to every aspect of his life. From methodically loading the dishwasher one way (and one way only) to organizing the kitchen junk drawer to perfection, he made sure his environment was consistent and controlled. He and my mom married when I was eight years old. The absolute predictability of his systems were a comfort initially as I rebounded from the chaos of my parents' divorce, but once I hit middle school, I rebelled against rigidity. Being micromanaged while loading a dishwasher is no fun for anyone, but to me it felt like the cruel stifling of my individuality. Sure, that sounds a bit dramatic, but I was a thirteen-year-old girl, so, you know, par for the course.

This is what an after-meal scene might have looked like at our house:

ME: *Puts plate in the dishwasher. Puts fork and knife in silverware basket. (A teenager doing chores? How could this not be great!)*

HIM: *Standing by the washer and watching me load my items.* That's not how it goes.

ME: What?

HIM: That's not how it goes.

ME: *In my head, "Who made you the boss of how it goes? Why does it have to be your way? Maybe there's a better way." And outside of my head,* "What?"

HIM: *Frustrated,* "You have to scrape the plate and it goes in the front facing forward."

ME: *In my head, "Then face it forward. Why should I have to do it? You have hands." And outside of my head,* "Fine."

For each additional dinner item, piece of silverware, cup, etc., he would stand there, hands on hips, watching me correct my mistakes until it was done correctly. The scene would end ten minutes later with me going to my room and shutting the door for the rest of the night.

The upside here, and it's no small one, is that under my step-father's watchful and insistent eye, I became a very hard worker. I don't give up when things get hard. I am persistent. I can work with people who require high standards of production. And if loading a dishwasher ever becomes an Olympic sport, I am sure to win a gold medal. All of these things I can attribute to my stepfather's influence and, truly, for these things I am grateful.

You know there's a "but" coming, right? *But,* despite some of the excellent outcomes of being micromanaged, it had its many drawbacks. I didn't like inviting friends to my house for fear they would be micromanaged (mortifying). I took more risks as a teen outside of the house because I couldn't take them at home. I lacked confidence.

It's hard to weigh the positive outcomes of the lessons I learned on dishwasher duty against the negatives. As an adult, I know that they aren't mutually exclusive. There are ways to teach necessary life skills and to set high standards while still encouraging creativity and individuality. Ask me today and I'll tell you unequivocally that the forks go in the dishwasher basket with the tines facing up. (Heck, don't ask me and I may tell you anyway. Sorry about that.) But if my kids load the dishwasher, run it, and then unload it when it's done, and I'm not standing over them micromanaging, I never have to know which way the tines faced. They get both the valuable life lessons that come from being self-sufficient and the satisfaction of having independently contributed to the family, and I get to watch *Project Runway* in the other room.

Anticipating the counterpoint that loading a dishwasher is one thing, but being strict about things like curfew, social media use, and homework are entirely another, I offer this: you should absolutely set limits on middle schoolers. Make them go to bed at a reasonable hour, make them do chores, and make them spend time with your family. Set your hard limits but pick your battles wisely. Like a good boss would, set clear expectations on defining success for your most important items, and for the rest, take a deep breath and look the other way.

Since you're now in the business of being an assistant manager rather than a micromanager, one of your key job functions is to help your child slow down her thinking process. This helps your child develop critical thinking and impulse control. A great way to slow down thinking is to help your child explore her options by asking nonjudgmental questions. I know that might sound like a soft approach, but it has terrific emotional and developmental advantages.

Imagine a scenario in which your son declares that he is quitting the basketball team because the coach is a total jerk. You know your son is overreacting because his "manager" is off duty and therefore his critical thinking, impulse control, and social behavior are not working properly. These are the very reasons you can't convince him to think about this situation differently. What you can do is ask him the kinds of questions that lead him to his own, better solution. For example:

- Is there anything about being on the team you would miss?
- How do the other kids react when the coach is being a jerk?
- What would you do differently if you were the coach?
- How do you think your teammates will react if you quit?

These questions stop the anger roll and get your son thinking about the situation, instead of reacting impulsively.

> Parents: Keep a neutral facial expression (no scrunched foreheads) when listening or talking to your middle schooler. This is important because your kid won't talk if he feels he's being judged. I call this having "Botox Brow," and it works wonders in keeping lines of communication open.

If you respond in any of the following ways, however, your son will likely shut down communication and stop talking:

- Quit?! Your teammates need you. You can't let them down!
- Oh, but you're a great basketball player! Don't quit. I love watching you play.
- He may not be the best, but he's your coach. In the real world, we all have to deal with irritating personalities.
- You're overreacting. Last week you had a great game. Just give it time and you'll get over it.

These responses don't help with your goal to slow down your son's thinking process or cause him to think more critically about the situation. They just complicate his world by adding in new elements (letting teammates down, letting you down, implying this affects his future, dismissing his feelings). He's likely to feel burdened and go "radio silent" rather than opening up and thinking through the problem more rationally.

Surprisingly, my stepfather was also a master at this type of questioning. I remember when my two best friends from middle school kicked me out of our social circle. I was devastated and he found me crying one day in our basement rec room. With his usual Spock-like logic, he began asking questions about my situation with no judgment or emotion detectable.

- Are you crying because you really want to be friends with them or are you sad that this happened?
- Do you respect them? If yes, take their criticism as helpful. If not, forget what they say.
- If you saw someone else in your situation, what would you say to her?

He didn't tell me they were terrible people. Had he, I would have defended them! He didn't tell me I should get over it because they aren't worth it. Had he, I would have cried harder because I didn't know how to get over them. What worked was that he slowed me down enough to begin thinking critically about the situation instead of emotionally, without pushing his opinions on me.

PRACTICE MAKES PERFECT

It's a cliché that when someone says something awful to you, two days later you'll come up with the perfect response. It's hard for most of us to immediately think of the right response to a strange social situation, but it's even harder for middle schoolers. When a friend criticizes them, or a popular girl asks to copy their homework, or a cute boy makes fun of their outfit, usually what comes next is a highly emotional response. Some kids cry easily, others comply quickly, others come out swinging, and others shut down completely. The best way to help your kid with these kinds of situations is to *practice how to respond ahead of time.*

Practicing responses to tough situations looks a little like role playing, but I'm reluctant to call it that because I don't imagine most kids being willing to act out awkward hallway moments with their parents. Think of it more as starting with those open-ended questions highlighted in the previous section and, as your child opens up, asking him to say out loud what his response would be.

There's more than one benefit to practicing these situations with your kids. For starters, it's the only way they won't be caught totally off guard while their "manager" is on break. For another, it's the best way to build critical thinking and problem-solving skills into their long-term brain function. At about the time your child goes to middle school, his temporal lobe, which is like a filing cabinet holding all the important learning he has accumulated through the years, begins to make room for all the new things he'll learn next.

> Twice in our lives, the temporal lobe purges information it deems unnecessary so it can make room for new information, roughly at ages two and eleven.

How does the brain decide what information it will clean out to make room for new knowledge? Quite simply. What is used the least, must go first. If your child stops practicing a certain skill, her brain will decide that skill can be flushed out to make room for something else.

This is significant to your parenting for two reasons:

1. If it is important to you or your kid to carry a skill into adulthood, don't let her quit before age eleven. I'm not saying don't

quit anything. Just evaluate what is most important (maybe playing an instrument or speaking a second language) and stick with it until age thirteen. From there, you can stop for a while and come back to it later without that knowledge being purged.

2. New skills being learned in adolescence will only be safely stored in your child's brain with heavy repetition and practice. This becomes very important to helping your child solve social problems. It's not enough to say, "Tomorrow, try standing up for yourself if you're teased on the bus." You need to practice with your child what to say, how to stand, and where to look, so your child will be able to do it on the spot. The more you practice, the more proficient your child will become.

HOW TO PRACTICE WITH YOUR KID

I run a summer camp for middle school girls called Athena's Path and one for boys called Hero's Pursuit. It's a weeklong program filled with games, activities, and lessons that help kids survive and thrive in the middle school social landscape. Thousands of kids go through the program, and the lesson that always hits home hardest is "Responding to Criticism," in which campers brainstorm *positive* ways to respond to destructive criticism. First, each camper writes the worst thing someone could say to or about her on an index card. Then, she develops her own positive response and practices the response in front of the group.

Ten years ago, in the first ever Athena's Path camp, a sweet girl named Laura★ who was heading into sixth grade wrote on her card, "You're weird and no one likes you." She bravely chose to use humor as her response should her hypothetical situation ever come true, and she practiced with the other campers. The first time she practiced,

---

★All names of tweens or teens in this book have been changed but their stories have not.

someone read Laura what she had written on her card and she didn't respond well. Her instinct was to insult the other person, so her reply came out something like, "Well, at least I have a life, unlike you." But her camp leader got her to try again, and again, until her response showed confidence without being so edgy that it would engage the other person in a fight. Laura landed on a humorous, "That's okay. Weird is working for me. Plus, it's all I have right now!"

According to her mom, neither Laura nor her mom really believed this exercise would be useful. Laura was a happy girl, a year-round athlete with a fun and supportive family, and she had plenty of success in elementary school. Once sixth grade began she was eager to start riding the bus to school. About a week into the school year, an eighth-grade girl stopped by her seat on her way to the back of the bus. Looking straight at Laura but talking loudly for the benefit of the whole bus, she asked, "What's the matter with your hair?"

Laura remembered practicing for this at camp. She smiled back and said, "I don't know but it's all I've got!" She passed the test, and the eighth grader kept moving to her seat without further incident. That afternoon, when Laura got off the bus, she saw her mom and burst into tears. According to her mom, Laura was stressed out for a few minutes, but pretty quickly calmed down and told her that she handled the problem herself with what she learned at camp. In this way, three great things came from Laura's experience.

1. She avoided an impulsive, emotional response that would have escalated the conflict.
2. By practicing her critical thinking and problem-solving skills, she helped cement them into her temporal lobe.
3. She increased her confidence in handling problems on her own and didn't become a victim.

Some parents confuse a planned, calm response with rolling over. They think a kid needs a tough attitude or a fighting comeback to win in these scenarios. In fact, this is far from the truth. Matching the attitude of the instigator only escalates conflict. What works is exuding confidence while appearing calm and unphased by the comments. After all, this is a true display of strength.

The obvious hang-up is that no middle schooler is naturally calm and unphased when being teased. This is why practice is essential. Explain all of this to your child. Ask her to come up with five different things she could say to a mean comment without escalating the situation toward a fight. Then, tell her to practice. Say, "Pretend I'm a kid on the bus and I say, 'Shut up. You're a loser.' What do you say back to me?" Don't pretend to be a middle schooler, overact, or make a big deal of it. If you stay emotionally neutral, she'll have more respect for the exercise because it won't feel "dorky."

The final key to teaching this to your child is not just covering what to say to an insult, but how to end a confrontation. Suggest closing statements like, "That's all" or "We have different opinions on this" (said casually, and even with a smile), and tell her to turn away or start walking. If she keeps standing there, the other person will continue to escalate the conflict.

EMPATHY: YOUR MIDDLE SCHOOLER'S SUPERPOWER

While it may be hard to see the positive side of living with someone whose managerial brain function is off duty, if you squint and look really hard you may be able to make out a rewarding upside after all.

During the tween and teen years, other parts of the brain have to step up and take a lead role while the prefrontal cortex is doing its job of getting stronger. Thus, the central part of the brain, the amygdala, takes the lead for our teens. It may come as no surprise that the amygdala is the *emotional* center of the brain.

On the downside, middle schoolers react with disproportionate emotion to seemingly small situations. On the upside, middle schoolers react with disproportionate emotion to social injustice. Have you ever met anyone more righteous or determined than a seventh grader who senses something is unfair?

One of the nicest things about the amygdala is that it houses empathy. Did you read a book in or around seventh grade that made you cry uncontrollably? For me, it was *The Autobiography of Miss Jane Pittman*. And *The Outsiders*. And about twenty others. There is something magical about the middle school years, when you believe wholeheartedly in the power of change and your ability to make a difference in the world. It's easy and understandable to be annoyed by the deluge of emotions in middle school. Let's also celebrate that this flood brings forth waves of empathy, which set your kid up to be a more compassionate and helpful member of society.

Your middle schooler's lack of judgment, and impulse control, and critical thinking, along with an overflow of emotions, will make for a bumpy ride sometimes. Try to enjoy the adventure and spontaneity of it all. I promise it doesn't last long.

Now that you have a basic understanding of how brain functions work and don't work during the middle school years, let's take a look at why that manager has to go on break anyway, and why for so *long*.

3

Middle School Requires Bravery

Sometime in the mid-eighties, I read an interview with Amy Grant in *Seventeen* magazine that had a profound impact on me. She said something like this: If you want to dye your hair purple and speak in a British accent, why not? It's not permanent. Have a little fun trying to figure out who you are.

As a teen, it was liberating to be told that I could sample styles, cultures, *and accents* even, to see what felt most like the me I wanted to be. Thus began a daring (and horrific) period of fashion in my life. From MC Hammeresque diaper pants to bad perms to lace gloves, I took every fashion risk imaginable in my quest to figure out *who I was.* Turns out, I'm your basic jeans and T-shirt kind of girl after all, but it was nice knowing I had the right to experiment before reaching a foregone conclusion.

We all know kids begin taking more risks in middle school. Certainly, not all the risks they take are as harmless or temporary as bad clothing, but the more we encourage these kinds of risks, the less likely it is that our kids will dabble in the categories of sex, drugs, and strangers that truly frighten us.

> Expecting our kids to take risks is one thing. Supporting them while they do it is another. The key to feeling supportive of, and not insulted by, your kid's new attitude is understanding what motivates this new behavior.

INDIVIDUALITY IS CRUCIAL

Remember, the prefrontal cortex (the manager of your kid's brain) isn't fully functional during the tween and teen years. You also now know that the emotional center of the brain steps into a lead role during this time, and that it's your job to be an "assistant brain manager" through high school, to help your kid develop critical thinking skills and impulse control. All of this seems like a pretty random and messy way to get through adolescence. Wouldn't it have made more sense for kids to have stronger impulse control through the teen years when they are more likely to get into trouble?

It's logical to think that way, but actually, there is an important reason the prefrontal cortex takes so long to fully form and the emotional center of the brain holds such power at this age.

> Your child's primary job beginning in middle school is to develop an identity apart from you.

Why? Because over the next eight years (a relatively long period now that was much shorter for our ancestors) your child will begin the process of preparing to leave your home. (I'm crossing my fingers for you.) He will no longer be grounded by your rules and influence. He needs to know who he is and what he stands for, not who *you* are and what *you* stand for, to make it out there.

This may not make sense at first. You may be wondering, do you really start developing an identity just because you go to sixth grade? Aren't you always a unique individual from the get-go?

You're right. Every child is born with a unique set of personality traits. My friend Dawn, a wonderful child psychologist, says that the parents' job is to create the best environment for the child they were given, not the child they expected. Parents start seeing temperament and unique personality traits in their offspring as early as infancy, but kids don't view themselves as autonomous individuals until much later. Little ones understand themselves to be extensions of their parents until about age twelve, at which time they begin questioning their parents in an attempt to figure out who they are apart from them.

This is an incredibly difficult challenge for a little one who has been tucked under your wing for the past twelve years or so—and, without a doubt, it can be hard on the parents as well. One way to prepare for this major shift is to give your child ample opportunity to begin asserting her uniqueness at a younger age. One of the ways I did this was through clothing.

My oldest child is a girl. When she was in preschool the fashion was smocked dresses and ridiculously large hair bows. I mean, I do not know how some of the girls in the preschool program kept their heads upright. I tried the smocked dress and hair bow thing a few times, but my girl just yanked that bow right out. I saw other girls doing the same, while moms pleaded, distracted, threatened, and punished if the bows didn't stay in place. It was weird how seriously the moms took their daughters' appearances and it was clear that they saw the girls as an extension of themselves, almost as an accessory. In the same way you wouldn't dress up in a fancy outfit and carry a plastic grocery bag for a purse, you wouldn't tote around a three-year-old dressed like a hobo. It simply wouldn't match.

Not only would my daughter not wear a hair bow, she would dress herself in bizarre combinations of clothing. Rain boots, a tutu, a shawl…and she was ready! I let her wear outfits that I found, well, really crazy. But I wasn't immune to what other people thought. In fact, I worried about their opinions of me as a mom even though I thought I was doing the right thing. There was still the fairly consistent voice in the back of my head that wondered if she would be a friendless cat lady later in life wearing high heels, a bathrobe, and a tiara because I never did the motherly thing and taught her what was fashion appropriate.

One of my happiest moments of her preschool years came one morning when my daughter was strutting into school in one of her doozies, and a mom of a beautiful and always well-matched little girl said to me, "I love seeing what she comes up with. One day, we're going to be buying her designs." With that, I was no longer filled with doubt. I felt a surge of pride that said, "*Yes!* This is how entrepreneurs and artists are made!"

The point is, if your first experience with letting your child assert her individualism doesn't come until middle school, you are both in for a painful time. Also, she may feel that if she can't express herself through her room décor, clothing, speaking, singing, writing, painting, or any other deeply personal and highly *public* form of self-expression, she will have to do it privately, as in, behind your back.

> Let your child be who she is out loud so that she doesn't need to experiment in sneaky ways.

THE MANAGER HAS LEFT THE BUILDING

Making personal choices is a big step toward independence. At the end of elementary school, your child is, hopefully, packing his own lunch, showering without much complaint, and generally helping you around the house when you ask. (If not, start today!) After so many years of needing your help with every little task, this burgeoning independence feels like the Promised Land. Ah, but you haven't arrived yet. There's a false sense of security that comes at the end of elementary school, but your middle schooler's task of building an identity is about to rock your world and his. Just remember, without this step in life, your child can't confidently answer the question, "Who am I?" So though this next stage may be bumpy, it's both necessary and ultimately very fulfilling.

The brain's manager, or prefrontal cortex, has the responsibility of controlling impulses and thinking critically. On the one hand, it sure would make parenting a tween much easier if these functions were fully active during the middle school years. On the other hand, it sure would make being a tween so much harder. Your tween's developmental responsibility is to form a unique identity apart from you so that she can leave your house, get a job, and start a family of her own someday. Her manager, however, would suggest that's not necessary. Its function is to help us play it safe, think reasonably, and not take unnecessary risks. The manager would whisper in her ear, "Why take a risk? You have everything you need *right here*. A warm bed, plenty to eat, TV. It's scary out there. Let's just stay put."

The next time you're feeling overwhelmed by your middle schooler's attitude or impulsiveness, take heart and remember that these behavior changes serve a higher purpose.

> Developing an identity requires one thing in spades that critical thinking and impulse control tend to squelch: bravery.

THE MIDDLE SCHOOL IDENTITY CRISIS

Psychologist Erik Erikson coined the phrase *identity crisis,* and central to a middle schooler's crisis is the difficulty of straddling childhood and adulthood. Does your daughter want to wear makeup one day and brush her doll's hair the next? Or does your son want to cuddle next to you on the couch one minute, but then snaps at you when you ask who he's texting? It's hard to figure out how to cross the bridge from childhood to adulthood. When your peers begin evaluating how well you're making that transition, it is even harder.

Around you, it's cool for your daughter to play with her dolls.

Around her friends, it's embarrassing. Around her frenemies, it's social suicide. Your daughter has to figure out who she is depending on *every* possible social context she may encounter. She has to develop a lot of theories about herself in the world and make a lot of assumptions to test those theories. "Who am I?" is an enormously difficult question in middle school, because there are so many possible answers.

If your child confides in you about a social dilemma and you reply, "Just be yourself," your child might well wonder, "Which me should I be? Should I be the *me* I am at the breakfast table at home, on the bus with the intimidating kids, suffering in math, scoring on the soccer field, watching someone being bullied, sharing secrets with my best friend after school, or cuddling with my mom?"

Each social context asks for a different response from your child. Sometimes the big kid shows up, sometimes the young adult. Until she figures out her true identity (and no one does that in middle school because this stage lasts throughout the teen years) there will be many missteps and mistakes along the way. It's supposed to be that way. Without the struggle, your child can't figure out who she is and will become.

"Just be yourself" is an incomplete answer to your child's social dilemmas. Begin by empathizing, as in: "That must have been hard (or disappointing) (or embarrassing)." Continue by explaining that you understand the pressure on your child to figure out how to act or feel in so many types of situations. That would be hard on anyone. Round it out by reassuring her that figuring her social scene out will sometimes be challenging and sometimes exciting, and that no matter what happens, you will be there for her without judgment.

So, what if your kid doesn't develop his own identity? What if he really likes being an extension of you and what if you don't particularly mind that? You love being so close! You have strong values and convictions, and if he feels in total agreement with you on those, what's wrong with him being a mini you?

Theoretically, there is nothing wrong with your middle schooler growing up under your roof and never challenging your authority and having opinions that agree with yours. Frankly, that sounds quite nice. Unfortunately, though, it doesn't often work that way. Your daughter doesn't have to do a complete 180 from your influence, and I hope she doesn't, but developmental stages aren't optional. You can't just chill there in one stage endlessly without any repercussions. Like a game of Sorry!, if you stay in one spot for too long, you're likely to get bumped out and the consequences can be ugly.

The developmental stage that begins in the middle school years is called Identity vs. Role Confusion. According to Erikson, this stage, like the seven others he identified from birth to death, is a time of life when each of us must resolve a conflict to successfully move on to the next stage. The conflict of Identity vs. Role Confusion is between wanting to be an individual and being confused about your role in the world. That definitely sounds like a teenager. People who don't develop a positive sense of identity still pass on to the next developmental stage, called Intimacy vs. Isolation, at around age nineteen. As the name of this stage clearly implies, this time of life (lasting through early adulthood until about age forty) is about resolving how to form rewarding, intimate relationships with other people or, if not, being alone.

The consequence of passing on to the Intimacy vs. Isolation stage without having a strong sense of self can be disastrous. I am reminded of the old Johnny Lee song "Looking for Love," as in "I was looking for love in all the wrong places, looking for love in too many faces." Young adults who don't have success resolving their Identity vs. Role Confusion conflict end up being more promiscuous and feeling more isolated and depressed than those who emerge from adolescence with a strong identity.

TAKING THE RIGHT RISKS

In order to develop an identity separate from you, your middle schooler should be taking more and more risks. As a parent, I know how unnerving it is to hear that but hopefully I've convinced you it's necessary.

Quick poll: *How many of you would like your child to live in her own house someday?* Everyone? Perfect.

The fact is that you have created a lovely beginning for your child, but you are not your child's future. Her future rests on how successfully she can navigate a world run by her peers. Figuring out how that social world will work and where she will fit into it is the key to your child's future success.

If only your child could just go into an empty room, shut the door, and emerge years later with a shiny new, terrific identity! But figuring out who you are is an enormously large *social* project. It involves moving from concrete to theoretical thinking—not an easy skill to master. Theoretical thinking is all about making assumptions to test theories. Your middle schooler's brain is working overtime to make a million assumptions about how the social world works and then seeing how people react to each and every one of those assumptions. This means trying new fashions, hairstyles, language, friends, bravado, and behavior on for size, as well as taking in every reaction—good and bad—to these changes as an indication of their success or failure in building an identity.

It is incredibly hard for kids to learn who they are and where they fit outside of "parent world." It will take some trial and error, many mistakes, and a dash of rebellion to leave your safe haven and strike out on their own.

WAYS YOU CAN HELP

As a parent of two middle schoolers, I know there are many occasions when you will feel frustrated by the influences of your child's peers and the broader culture on your family's happiness. Thankfully, there are many simple ways you can abate that feeling of helplessness as you support your tween on the rocky road from little kid to adult. I've listed my favorites here.

Help Your Child Take Risks

Create an atmosphere where your child is allowed to do things that feel thrilling, daring, scary, and unknown. When you fill that need for risk with a positive source, there is less chance your child will try to fill it through unhealthy activities. You might encourage:

- Auditioning for a play or commercial
- Starting a business
- Trying a new sport (rock climbing, white-water rafting, etc.)
- Getting a part-time job
- Running for student council
- Joining or starting a club
- Entering a competition
- Joining Scouts
- Starting a blog
- Mentoring a younger child
- Volunteering at an animal shelter

Rebellion is a critical step in finding individuality, but I'm not suggesting you applaud when you catch your kid smoking behind the middle school. How you react to your child's missteps will set him up for one of two things: more success or more failure.

Express Empathy

Whether it is a bold act of rebellion or an awkward stumble onto the wrong path, when your child makes a mistake, express empathy first. "That must have been hard or painful or embarrassing," always comes before, "You screwed up; how are you going to fix it?" React in the way you would like your spouse, partner, or friend to react when you make a mistake. Yes, you're the parent, and as a parent it's part of your job to model empathy before launching into discipline.

Be Unemotional in Your Discipline

You may cry into your own pillow at night if you need to, but if you cloud your discipline with tears, anger, or despair in front of your child, she will likely misinterpret you. Be firm, direct, and without emotion when talking about consequences. If you need to buy some time to achieve this say something like, "I need some time to figure out how to respond. I'll talk to you about this tonight after dinner."

The next time you feel frustrated or betrayed by your middle schooler's attitude, imagine the alternative. He could *not* rebel, *not* stretch to figure out his new identity within his peer world, and remain perfectly comfortable staying under your roof... for the next forty years or so.

Motivate with Social Reward

Adults usually think kids take risks because they weren't thinking. Actually, middle schoolers have a good understanding of the potential dangers behind the risks they take. So why do they do such crazy and careless things?

A 2007 study by Laurence Steinberg at Temple University[1] found that teens clearly do understand what might happen when they binge drink, jump off a cliff, or text with a stranger (for example). In fact, they evaluate risk about as effectively as adults. So what incentivizes them to engage in such risky behavior anyway?

> Tweens and teens overvalue the reward that comes from risk, particularly when the reward may add to their social standing.

While adults can say, "I'm not going to drink and drive because I could hurt myself or someone else," an adolescent will think, "I shouldn't drink and drive because I could hurt myself or someone else. But, it's worth taking the risk because those jocks are watching me and they might think I'm cooler if I do it." I've simplified that because it's more a feeling than an expressive thought. Earning social credentials trumps the fear of getting in trouble or getting hurt.

Understanding what motivates your child is a key to good parenting because you can use that to your advantage. Sneaky, huh? Middle school is a great time to begin using social rewards as incentives because kids value this above most other things. Want your child to get a good grade on her upcoming test? Dangle a carrot. Offering her a sleepover if she gets above a ninety will motivate her much more than threatening to ground her if she gets below a seventy. You can even do both, but don't forget to include social rewards. Even more effective, ask your child to name a few social rewards that would excite him (time with friends at the mall, sleepovers, a night at the skating rink, and so on). When your kid is invested in choosing his rewards, he'll be more motivated to achieve his goals.

If you have a highly social child, you have already seen that clamping down on her social outlets doesn't work to motivate her. You may take away her phone, limit screen time, or ground her from going to social or sporting events, but she probably still finds a way to be social. She ends up talking more in class or sneaking hits of social media when you're not looking. It's as if she's starved for social contact.

My friend Rachel has a daughter, Alison, who is off-the-charts social. She is an incredibly likeable and attractive girl. I don't mean pretty, although she is. I mean people are attracted to her and want to spend time with her. She is a good and loyal friend and is highly active in her church youth group and sports teams. She loves being with other people! Sometimes, this causes a problem. Not infrequently, Alison gets into trouble at school for talking too much during class. It is frustrating for her teachers, who need to control the classroom climate for the overall good of the group.

What choice does her teacher have in getting Alison to be less social during class time? Well, he could sit her in the back of the class, perhaps at a desk separated from others, so she won't talk. But I know for a fact that wouldn't stop Alison. She would be secretly texting, or passing notes, or using sign language if she had to, in order to communicate with kids across the aisle. He could threaten her with a punishment if she spoke out. He's actually tried this before. The result is that Alison talked too much anyway and ended up at silent lunch, right next to her best friend, where they ate together and whispered under their breath. It was kind of fun.

The other option would be to dangle a social reward. The teacher might say to Alison, "If you only talk this period after you've raised your hand, and don't have side discussions with your friends, I'll allow you to pick a partner and work on the next project as a team. Otherwise, you'll have to work on it alone." Punishment doesn't deter Alison, but an opportunity to be more social, now that's exciting to her and she'll work hard for that. Of course, there are times when punishments are necessary. Kids need to learn consequences. But if motivation is your goal, think about whether punishment or social rewards will work best for your child.

For the child who isn't terribly social, do social motivators still work? Sometimes. Every kid's social needs are different. While a sleepover with three friends might sound like a blast to some kids, to others it would be overwhelming. Social rewards can come in many packages. Maybe it's a big group activity, one-on-one time with a friend, or getting a FaceTime account to chat with cousins from out of town; or maybe it's a new piece of clothing that adds social clout to your kid's wardrobe. Your child may be an introvert, but some aspect of being part of the middle school tribe may still motivate him. If you're sure this wouldn't motivate your child, spend some time observing what delights him and use that as an incentive.

Middle school requires bravery in many ways, not only from your kids. This is new territory for you, and in it you must conquer new ways of thinking, new approaches to parenting, even new ways of looking at your own personal evolution now that your kids are older. Be brave!

4

Talking with Your Middle Schooler, or Not

There is an almost mythic quote in the parenting world, often attributed to Mark Twain, although it's not his and no one knows who really said it. Nonetheless, it's a terrific characterization of the evolving parent–child relationship through the teen years: "When I was a boy of fourteen, my father was so ignorant I could hardly stand to have the old man around. But when I got to be twenty-one, I was astonished at how much he had learned in seven years."

One of the biggest complaints I hear from parents of tweens is that they miss a personal connection with their kids. It's terribly frustrating, even heartbreaking at times, to crave information about your child's world and to have your attempts at conversation stonewalled. Sometimes I feel like I'm watching my own children guest star in an episode of a familiar sitcom. I know exactly what's going to happen, I foresee every miscommunication and every missed opportunity, and I'm wriggling in my seat, bursting at the seams with advice that I know, if only they would listen, could clear up everything so neatly . . . but they can't hear me.

The good news is that communication during the middle school years doesn't go away, as long as you let it evolve. When your child was a toddler you probably got into the habit of dispensing a lot of information. Communication involved you labeling your child's world, identifying colors, numbers, and objects to build his vocabulary and concrete thinking skills, and him repeating those classifications back to you. Through elementary school, he began building more complex conversational patterns and became quite good at wondering, questioning, and engaging in two-way conversations where you both shared and absorbed information. But by middle school, the conversations become strange. They either stop altogether or become so one-sided about them that you wish sometimes they *would* stop.

There is, however, an effective and easy way to evolve your conversation skills again so that you can accommodate your kid's changing brain and get him to engage with you pleasantly once more. It's a method I call "Botox Brow."

Don't worry (or get excited, as the case may be), I am not suggesting you stick a needle in your forehead in order to have a better relationship with your middle schooler. (If you want to do that for your own reasons, have at it!) What I am suggesting is simply a metaphor for a much less painful approach to communicating with your child.

My "Botox Brow" method of communication is rooted in this assumption: *Your child thinks you're angry when you're not.* Dr. Deborah Yurgelun-Todd, former director of neuropsychology and cognitive neuroimaging at McLean Hospital (an affiliate of Harvard Medical School), performed groundbreaking research into how adolescents read facial expressions.[1]

Turns out, adolescents are terrible at reading facial expressions. They often perceive you to be angry when you aren't. Do yourself a favor and keep a neutral facial expression when talking to your middle schooler.

Yurgelun-Todd showed pictures of faces expressing distinct emotions to both adults and teens, and used MRI scans to determine which part of the brain they used to identify emotions by reading facial expressions. She saw that adults used the prefrontal cortex (hello again!) to decipher people's expressions and then to correctly guess what that person was feeling based on his facial expressions. Adults in this study correctly labeled emotions about 90 percent of the time. Teens, however, don't use their still-forming prefrontal cortex to identify people's emotions. Instead, they rely on the limbic area, which is the emotionally charged hot seat in the brain (hello again!), and clearly not the best place to gather information. The emotion that registers most prominently in a teen's brain? Anger. While an adult can differentiate between pictures of people who look angry, scared, or shocked, teens almost always guess that the person feels *angry*.

How does this impact your parenting? Understanding that your child can't read facial expressions accurately should change the way you look when you talk to your middle schooler. Let's say your child comes to you with news that he was teased at school. You may have an expression of concern, sympathy, or shock. Unless your face is totally neutral, your child will likely interpret your response as anger. Next, he will stop telling you personal things for fear you will get mad. This is a no-win situation.

Your child's inability to read facial expressions has probably led to some awkward conversations at your house. For instance, how many times have you had a conversation like this?

YOUR KID: Evan called me the b-word today.
YOU: *What?!* (You are shocked and concerned)
YOUR KID: Oh my God! You don't have to get mad at *me* about it!

Anytime you simply furrow your eyebrows, you run the risk of your child thinking you're angry. Why is this a risk? As soon as your child thinks you're angry, she clams up and you can no longer help her. Tweens are highly sensitive to feeling "judged" and they shut down the second they think you're disappointed or angry.

Instead, when your child comes to you with a situation, keep a totally neutral face. This is what I call having "Botox Brow," no furrowed brow, no big eyes, no expression whatsoever.

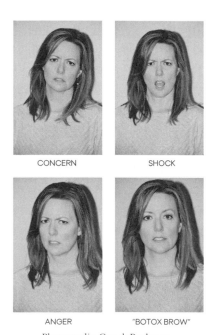

CONCERN   SHOCK

ANGER   "BOTOX BROW"

Photo credit: Gareth Rasberry

Want your kid to share more and be more receptive?
Use the "Botox Brow" expression with your middle schooler to
promote better conversations.

Even though I'm feeling different emotions in all four of these
photos, my kids think I'm angry in three of them. The more neutral
I look, the more they open up. I know, it sounds weird. But it *works*.
As soon as you employ the "Botox Brow" when talking to your middle schooler about anything social, you will find the conversations
are much more pleasant and productive.

SAY WHAT YOU FEEL

If step one is to keep a neutral expression when communicating
about topics with your child, step two is to *say* what you feel, instead
of showing it on your face. I'm not saying you can't get upset when

you hear bad news. I'm just saying that if the door to communication opens, don't risk your kid misinterpreting how you feel. In the same scenario as before, here is how "Botox Brow" would work:

> YOUR KID: Evan called me the b-word today.
> YOU: (with a neutral face) I'm so sorry. That's shocking. You okay?
> YOUR KID: Yes, he's just a jerk!
> YOU: What did you say?
> YOUR KID: I didn't say anything. I was too shocked. But Mr. McNeely heard, so he got in trouble. (The conversation continues, with you getting a lot more information than in the first example.)

Along with a neutral face, keep your voice as neutral as possible. You might feel a little like a Stepford parent at this point, a robot underneath a pretty exterior, especially if, like me, you enjoy being expressive when you talk. I have big eyes and I wave my hands around a lot. But when I'm talking to my kids about what's happening in their lives, I tone it all down. When they don't feel judged, they're more comfortable sharing information.

CAN'T I EVER JUDGE?

Although I'm advocating a neutral *expression* when communicating with your tweens, I'm not suggesting you have to *be* neutral on issues that cause you concern about morality or safety. Once you begin practicing "Botox Brow" and your kid starts opening up to you, you're going to hear a few things that are exciting, a lot of things that are boring and self-indulgent, and a few things that are upsetting. What do you do about the upsetting things?

A parent once said to me, "But I'm the parent. It's my job to be judgmental of my kids." Oh, boy. I think some parents confuse judgment with discipline, so let's dissect these two. At the risk of sounding like an eighth-grade language arts paper, to pass judgment is defined by the *Oxford English Dictionary* as to "criticize or condemn someone from a position of assumed moral superiority." The goal of judgment is either to make other people feel badly about themselves or to make you feel better about yourself. Pause for a moment and think of the best teacher you ever had. Didn't he or she make you feel good about yourself? It's difficult to learn when you feel like you're operating from a position of assumed inferiority.

On the other hand, *discipline,* according to the *Oxford English Dictionary,* means to "train (someone) to obey rules or a code of behavior, using punishment to correct disobedience." The goal of discipline is to inspire better behavior. The word discipline is actually derived from the Latin *discipulus,* meaning "learner," and *discere,* meaning "to learn." As parents, it should be our goal to teach our children how they can be successful once they leave our care. Rabbi Shmuley Boteach, a parenting and relationship educator, once said, "Parenting is done with two hands—the right hand is unconditional love, and the left hand is establishing boundaries amidst that unconditional love. That is the role of a parent—love and discipline." In this formula, there is no room for judgment because that would only suffocate your best intentions.

Which brings us back to that awkward moment, after you've been successfully practicing "Botox Brow" and nonjudgmental reactions, when your tween reveals to you a situation that makes your skin crawl or your blood boil. What do you do?

1. Take a deep breath. This is an overused phrase, and an underpracticed one, too.
2. Buy yourself some time. You don't have to react right away. Say, "This is going to take a minute for me to think through. Can I get back to you tonight?" Walk away.

3. Think about the outcome you most want. What do you need to teach your child about this? Work backward to figure out the best way to teach that.

When you don't know what to say, be quiet.

UNBREAKABLE RADIO SILENCE

You may have tried everything you can think of, including my "Botox Brow" technique, and still your kid just won't open up. You've read the right books and blogs. You've asked questions a thousand different ways. You've offered to take your kid shopping or out for ice cream to persuade communication. You've tried every trick in the book, but your kid still won't tell you anything about what's going on in middle school. Short of waterboarding, you're not sure how to get this kid to spill some secrets.

Whenever I talk with a group of parents, this is a concern from at least one person in the audience, who is probably vocalizing what twenty more parents are feeling. One of the more frustrating aspects of parenting middle schoolers is that you really do want to help, and sometimes they make it really hard for you to do that.

When parents ask me what they can possibly do to get their tight-lipped kids to talk with them, my answer is, "Probably nothing." You can't force someone to talk any more than you can force someone to eat. Eventually, if you're patient, it will happen. Or it won't. This is just one of those things in life you can't control. But while you're busy tapping your foot and listening to the sound of silence, here are some things for your consideration and to ease your mind.

It really is normal (emotionally and developmentally) for your kid to clam up around this time. I want you to understand some things about communication with your kid during these years:

- It's appropriate for your kid to tell you less and less about her personal life. Don't beat yourself up if she doesn't want to share.
- You can't force a kid to talk to you. Even if you could bring words out of his mouth, you can't guarantee what he says will be honest and meaningful. Don't try too hard.
- Some kids are never going to be effusive. This has nothing to do with you. Don't take it personally.

One of the most important safety nets you can create for your child during the radio silent years is a village. When my kids were in early elementary school, I told them which of my friends they could go to for anything they needed. "If you ever have questions you don't feel comfortable asking me, or if you are stuck somewhere and need a ride, or if you feel scared, you can talk with _____." When they got their first cell phones, I made sure these numbers were among the first we programmed in. Let your village know you're relying on them. And be part of the village for your friends. We've lost a little of this today and it may not happen naturally. Some people are afraid of "sticking their noses where they don't belong." Have a conversation with your closest friends about being the village through the middle school years. No matter how awesome you are, your child may not call you if there is beer at a party and he wants to leave. But he may call your friend, especially if your friend has encouraged your child on the side to make that call.

I have a friend who texts my middle school daughter from time to time about the boy my daughter likes. Another takes her to Marshall's every so often to browse the racks and chat. (I *hate* shopping so this is a double favor for me.) Her aunt takes her to Target and talks about reality TV. I know that when my daughter isn't talking to me, we'll have a community of strong women to carry us through the quieter years.

If your kid isn't completely tuned out, there are some things you can do to keep the lines of communication open.

• Play to your kid's strengths by asking for advice. Tweens, boys especially, love to solve problems. Being vulnerable with your kid and asking for help sets your kid up to do the same with you. I'm not suggesting you open up your personal life too wide. Don't talk about a fight you had with your partner, for example. But you might say something like, "I was in a meeting and someone cut me off and dismissed my idea. How would you have handled that?"

• Ask about talking later instead of springing a conversation on your kid, as in, "After dinner can I get ten minutes of your time to talk about the day? I just want to hear what's going on and get your opinion on some things." Some older kids feel ambushed when you ask them to stop what they're doing and sit down to talk. Give them a long heads-up for a smoother start.

• Give without expecting anything in return. If you model vulnerability with your child, you can't expect him to instantly give that back. You wouldn't give someone a present and then quickly ask, "Now what did you get me?" In the same way, it's not effective to share something personal with your son and then say, "Okay, now you tell me something." In time, he'll return the gift.

• Use social media to have fun or meaningful conversations. Ask questions about images or posts that looked interesting to you. "I saw you posted a picture on Instagram of the band One Republic. Did you hear they're coming to town this fall?"

• Talk with kids on the social media/technology platform of their choice. Try texting your kid the things you want him to know or remember, rather than bombarding him with a list when he walks in the door. Texting is probably how he communicates with everyone!

• Keep it casual. Sitting down and making eye contact is a total conversation killer with some kids. Take a walk, ride a bike, chop vegetables, play video games, or help him put away laundry, then casually strike up a conversation.

• Dangle a carrot. Is your kid begging to see a movie, read a book, or play a game you've held out on? Agree, based on the condition she discusses it with you before or after. I might say, "I'm not crazy about that movie because it looks like the female characters are treated really badly, but I'll agree to let you go if you agree to talk with me about it after." Yes, it's a form of bribery but who cares? You've got them right where you want them, to talk about your family values or some of the bigger issues happening in our culture. It's also an opportunity for you to demonstrate that you don't get emotional when discussing hot-button issues. This buys you a bit more trust.

• Create space for your kid's friends in the conversation. Your daughter may be unwilling to talk with you these days, but her friends probably aren't. In fact, they may not be talking to *their* parents, but to you, they're wide open! Include your kid's friends for dinner, take them on trips, and drive them places they want to go. Not only will you overhear some enlightening things, but you can also engage your kid's friends like you can't your own child. Bonus, when your daughter sees you not overreacting to a friend who lets it slip that she has a boyfriend, you've earned that much more credibility with your own kid for future conversations.

• Take advantage of bedtime. There is still something magical about tucking a tween into bed and having some one-on-one time. Kids are especially receptive to this talk time if they feel they're working the system. Chatting past official bedtime feels like bending the rules so they're more likely to keep the conversation going. Having a routine, whether bedtime talk, Sunday bike rides, or a Saturday morning Starbucks run will help, too.

Is your child still quiet? Unless your child is showing signs of depression (in which case, consult a doctor), go find something fun to do and wait this out. Sometimes kids feel too much pressure from their parents to be connected, talk it out, carry the family conversation, so they clam up completely.

> If your kid senses that you or your happiness depends too much on him, he may begin to pull away.

Think about this for a minute: Do you have hobbies, interests, and enjoyment outside of your children? If you don't have a happy list of things to do this month, make one. As your child sees you enjoying life outside of him, he will start to open up to you more and more.

Sometimes parenting a tween looks a lot like pretending you don't care. No one, especially middle schoolers, wants to feel their decisions or experiences are directly tied to your happiness. If you can create space at home where they feel safe to talk without judgment, you don't have to sacrifice communication through the middle school years.

As a parent who had been using my "Botox Brow" technique once said to me, "[They're] almost like cats...treat them with a slight indifference and they warm right up to you. Works in my house!"

While this may seem like a simple modification, using "Botox Brow" is a profound tool that will keep your child talking with you at a time when she is naturally starting to pull away. It gives you the opportunity to stay in touch with what's really happening in her world, to help her practice critical thinking and slow down impulse control, and to take your relationship to the next stage of development, where she begins to solve her problems independently using you as a sounding board rather than a crutch.

5

It's Not Your Problem

Did you see the movie *The Hurt Locker* starring Jeremy Renner as Sergeant First Class William James? Sergeant James's job is to diffuse bombs in a highly volatile and chaotic war environment, to save his own life and those of his fellow soldiers. Under normal circumstances, Sergeant James is a provocative, agitated, need-for-speed kind of guy. But he is just the man you want on your side when the situation becomes a matter of life or death. When he needs to, he channels his frenetic energy with intense focus and calm, blocking out all distractions—even fear.

You are going to encounter a lot of potentially explosive situations as a middle school parent. How you approach them could cause your child to blow up or, alternately, quietly diffuse. Remember, you're working with a child whose emotional center of the brain has taken control of her thoughts and actions. She is temporarily more impulsive and reactive than normal. She may cry, scream, become cold as steel, or drop on the floor in hysterical laughter at the slightest event. For the next few years, think of yourself as Sergeant James. When a potentially explosive situation presents itself, don't throw fuel on her fire. It may be gratifying in the moment to create fireworks, but in the long run, you only end up covered in shrapnel. Instead, approach your lovely little time bomb with intentional calm and focus, so that things don't blow up bigger than they should.

My friend Heather is the kind of parent who responds calmly to the wildest provocations. One day she told me about an incident with her son, Drake, that has inspired me ever since. This is a story that could have gone in ten different bad directions, but Heather diffused the situation with ease. One morning in the spring, Drake stayed upstairs longer than usual on a school morning. She called to him to hurry up. Casually, he told his mom that there was no school that day. It was a teacher workday, he promised, and he didn't need to go to school.

Heather, having more than one child, knew this could not possibly be true. Her daughter stood dressed for school, lunch packed and backpack filled. And so she was presented with an interesting dilemma. She began by asking Drake to clarify why he thought school was canceled, to which he replied with a series of "dumb and unrelated reasons that didn't make any sense."

Imagine all the ways in which this scenario might have played out in different homes. Let's have a little "Choose Your Own Adventure" fun with this one and look at some possible outcomes.

Do you:

A. Call Drake out for obviously lying and make him march upstairs to get ready?
B. Give up and let Drake stay home because maybe something is bothering him at school?

If you chose option A: In a loud and frustrated tone, with a furrowed brow, you tell Drake you're not buying what he's selling, and that if he doesn't get ready in the next five minutes, you're taking away his electronics for two weeks. Drake, who truly believes he's made a compelling case, becomes indignant. He argues with surprisingly bad logic and equally astounding tenacity. For fifteen minutes you are debating, then arguing, then yelling. Your daughter is whining about her brother making her late. Eventually, you get out the door but Drake ends up grounded, you end up going into work late, and everyone is angry.

If you chose option B: You tell Drake you don't think that's right;

there must be school today. He insists, offering more and more bad evidence to back up his claim. You sympathize because everyone has a bad day sometimes. You agree that he can stay home today but *just this once.* Drake smiles and heads upstairs to watch TV. Your daughter cries out, "Then I don't have to go either!" and you begin to feel very stressed. You tell your daughter she is already ready and to get in the car. She screams, "Not fair!" and won't speak to you the entire way to school. You get to work on time and in a terrible mood.

Neither option sounds particularly satisfying. Once a child reaches middle school, two things happen that make these types of scenarios so complicated. First, he begins learning how to use hypothetical thinking skills. In elementary school, he was mostly a concrete thinker, but now he is starting to think about concepts abstractly. This means he will come up with a lot of hypotheses about the world and test them to see what's true. When it comes to arguing, he will seem like a very, very bad lawyer. Instead of looking at evidence and then drawing a conclusion, his cases begin with a conclusion and then he creates a lot of supporting evidence for his claim that may or may not fit. Eventually, he'll learn how to work in the opposite order, but for now, his arguing skills will frustrate you beyond words.

Second, he is growing into an adult-sized body. He is so physically big now that you may not be able to *make* him do anything. He may respect you enough to eventually respond to your orders, but if he chooses to move slowly or not all, there isn't a whole lot you can do about it. Gone are the days when you could pick your child up and put him in the car when he fell down in a tantrum. At age twelve, however, if your son refuses to get in the car, you might be out of luck. Honestly, even if your son were small enough for you to pick up and put in the car, how weird would that be?

Which leaves you with only one choice. A secret option I didn't offer you because I wanted you to see how poorly A and B played out. Let's look at option C.

Option C in this scenario is the one my friend Heather picked and, like Sergeant James, she diffused her bomb quickly and calmly. Option C is to outsmart the kid.

This is how option C looked at Heather's house:

Drake says he is not going to school. Heather pauses for a moment and appears to think hard. "Wow. That's an interesting decision," she says calmly. "Huh."

"What?" he asks.

"No, nothing," she replies, with a neutral expression and a calm voice. "I just...you know, I'm not sure what the punishment would be for that one. School is definitely on today, so I won't debate that with you. I guess I'll have to spend some time thinking what the right consequence would be for this one since it's so unusual. Okay." (Remember, if you don't know what to say, don't say anything!)

"Ugh!" Drake exclaims. "You'll probably make me skip Nick's party this weekend or something! Fine, I'll go!"

"Okay," Heather said, and that was that.

She told me that, in truth, she had no intention of making her son skip the party but once he jumped to that conclusion she let it work in her favor. Of course, there was a chance her son would have stayed home after all, at which point, she really would have been forced to come up with a consequence. But, as a Love & Logic parenting class instructor, she is pretty good at those! The best thing she did was let her son come to his own conclusions. Like taking a leap of faith, this is a scary thing to do, but the timing is right in middle school and you usually land where you should.

STOP SOLVING YOUR KID'S PROBLEMS

We all want our kids to grow up to be expert, creative problem solvers. Like anything else in life, this requires some practice. To be perfectly clear, this requires problems on which to practice.

Wishing your child a middle school experience that is free of emotional pain and conflict is, in my opinion, a waste of a wish. This is not only because it's impossible, but because your child needs to bump up against some walls, however bruising that may be, to learn how to solve problems well. Not to mention, developing an identity is as much about figuring out who you aren't as who you are.

> One of the biggest, most important, and hardest paradigm shifts that comes with parenting a middle schooler is that you should no longer solve their problems for them.

When your daughter was little you always tied her shoes, and then you taught her how to do it herself. You always cut your son's food, and then you taught him how to do it himself. Little by little, you gradually and happily turned over the reins of self-care to your child.

It's easy to do with things like shoes and steak, but with social issues, not so much. Perhaps it's because no one has given you a step-by-step plan for how to do it. If you Google "how to tie your shoes" or "how to cut steak" you get a multistep, easy-to-follow plan and often a YouTube video to boot. Google "how to teach my daughter to handle gossip" or "how to help my son deal with that guy who tripped him in the hall" and it's not so cut and dry.

The most effective way to teach kids to solve their own problems is to first realize: it's their problem to solve. You may want to swoop in and make it better. You may be able to clearly see the quickest path to resolution, but remember: it's not your problem. It's also not nearly as simple as tying shoes or cutting steak. Suddenly, your child is worrying about a girl in class with cut marks on her arm, a boy who makes rude sexual comments, getting invited to the right party, or making the sports team. As parents, we may fear that because these problems are so serious, we *should* solve them for our kids, when truly we can't. And when we try, we do our kids the disservice of denying them problem-solving practice.

Imagine your daughter comes to you, teary eyed, and says she saw a picture posted online of her friends at a sleepover. Clearly, she was not invited. To make it worse, she heard them discussing it and when she asked what they were talking about, they said they were just joking; there was no sleepover. With this new evidence, her heart is broken and yours is, too.

There are many ways parents unintentionally sabotage their children at crucial moments like these. Here are a few:

Problem Solving To Don'ts

Don't skip empathizing and go straight into problem-solving mode. Have you ever confided in your spouse, partner, or friend, only to have him rush into fixing the problem before you've had a chance for a little pity? We all like to have our troubles acknowledged. Before anything else, be sure to address your child's feelings with something brief but heartfelt like, "I'm so sorry you're going through this" or "That must really hurt."

Don't suggest a solution that would work for you. Everyone is different. You might think a special night with mom getting manicures will soften the blow. Or, perhaps you're ready to pick up the phone and chew the other parents out. These might make you feel better if you were in her shoes, or in the moment as her mom, but remember, it's not your problem. It's up to her to choose a course of action that makes her feel better.

Don't blow it off. Whether your intentions are to show her that she deserves better or to distract her from the situation, downplaying what happened does neither. It only suggests that her feelings aren't valid, and she'll begin to tell herself that she is less than those other girls.

> Take your kid's problems seriously, just not personally.

When your child is being teased or excluded, you might want to march into the situation and take care of business (à la *The Hand That Rocks the Cradle*) or tuck your child under your wing and hide her from danger. But, at best, you're just applying a Band-Aid and at worst you're making her more of a target and undermining her confidence in her ability to take care of herself.

Despite your desire to mop up the floor with those kids who can be deceptive or outright nasty, it is in your best interest, as well as your child's, to stay calm. As your kid encounters social problems in middle school, try to remember these benefits to staying neutral in your kid's social scene:

- The lines of communication stay open between you and your kid because he can tell you anything without feeling judged.
- You instill confidence and high self-esteem because your kid believes she can take care of herself.
- You help your kid build better critical-thinking and problem-solving skills.
- Your kid doesn't blame you for suggesting the wrong solution to her problem.
- Your kid sees you modeling how to stay calm during a crisis.
- You maintain an ongoing dialogue about the situation rather than a one-shot response.
- Your kid has more ownership of the solution if she decides on her own how she wants to handle and implement it.

> Don't just talk about your middle schoolers' problems. Teach them how to solve them.

In this chapter, I'll explain how to teach your child a problem-solving skill set that will work for any problem. As with all skills, your child will get better, and more confident, at making decisions and handling situations as he practices these steps. These will come in handy since you just learned why you shouldn't solve his problems anymore! Before we launch into the problem-solving process, however, you'll need to get some buy-in from the other half of this equation, your kid.

Step 1: Introduce the idea before there's a problem. One evening at bedtime, or in the car, or wherever you do your best talking together, explain to your kid that he's getting old enough for you to let him solve a lot of his problems on his own. Tell him that doesn't mean you aren't interested and that you won't help, just that you'll give him more power in problem situations. Tell him you read about a new way to help people solve problems and you'd like to try it sometime with him.

Step 2: Promise to stay calm. You promise to stay calm no matter what he tells you is happening in school, at sports, or with friends, frenemies, or straight-up enemies.

Step 3: Promise he doesn't have to take action. You also promise not to make him do anything after he tells you what's happening. His only responsibility to you is to talk openly.

Step 4: Get his buy-in. Ask your kid if, under these circumstances, he would be willing to let you know the next time something is bothering him. Chances are good he'll be pretty excited about the promise of more power and you not flipping out, and he'll agree. Then, just leave it alone for a while. Soon, your kid will come to remind you of your promises or you'll sense something is wrong and you can remind him yourself.

Remember, sometimes the best time to address a problem isn't during the heat of the moment. A "heads-up" goes a long way toward willing participation. When your child is emotionally distressed by a problem, offer to help him right away or to spend some time relaxing together first. He may need to cool off before he can brainstorm. You can say something like, "I'll be reading in bed around nine o'clock if you want to come read by me or talk." Of course, when your timing includes pushing bedtime back your kid suddenly becomes much more talkative. You can use this to your advantage.

Once your kid has agreed to try the problem-solving process, and you've waited until a problem arises, it's time to put these steps into practice. Below are two sample scenarios, starting with a basic problem and then tackling a more complex emotional issue.

Sample Scenario 1

Step 1: Your kid comes to you with a problem.

> SON: Mom, I broke Anna's calculator today.

Step 2: You show some empathy.

> MOM: Oh, no. That's too bad. Sorry that happened. How did you feel?
> SON: Embarrassed!

Step 3: You ask him to list some ideas for how he could solve the problem. No matter what, don't judge any of the ideas. Just listen and ask for more ideas.

> SON: Well, I could buy her a new one.
> MOM: Okay. What else?
> SON: I could let her borrow mine when she needs one.
> MOM: Okay. Anything else?
> SON: I could tell her I'm sorry and see if she has a backup calculator.
> MOM: Yeah. Any other ideas?

And so on, until you have a list of options to choose from. For most of us, our best ideas are stuck behind our worst. The longer we brainstorm, the more clever our solutions become.

Step 4: Your son has exhausted his idea collection so you ask him to pick his two favorite ideas and imagine what would happen if he tried them. This seems tedious, but your kid's brain can't correctly estimate outcomes unless he thinks through the plan step by step.

> MOM: You've got lots of ideas to choose from. That's great. Which two are your best options?
>
> SON: Either buy her a new calculator or let her borrow mine.
>
> MOM: Okay. What would happen if you bought her a new one?
>
> SON: I'd have to spend money and I don't have any, so can you give me some?
>
> MOM: As a loan. And then what?
>
> SON: Then I'd have to go to the store, get a calculator, pay you back, and hand it to her in class.
>
> MOM: Would that make you feel less embarrassed?
>
> SON: Yes.
>
> MOM: Cool. How about your other idea to let her borrow yours? How would that work?
>
> SON: I would just let her borrow mine.
>
> MOM: Would there be times when you both need it at the same time?
>
> SON: Yes.
>
> MOM: How would you deal with that?
>
> SON: I don't know.
>
> MOM: Would this make you feel less embarrassed?
>
> SON: I'd be more embarrassed if I had to tell her she couldn't borrow it 'cause I was using it already.
>
> MOM: Okay. Do you like one idea better than the other?
>
> SON: Yes, I'll buy her a new one.

Step 5: Tell him he did a great job solving that problem and ask him to let you know how it goes.

> MOM: Sounds like a good solution to me. I can take you to the store later tonight. Let me know if she seems cool with it.
> THE END

You don't have to use this process for every problem. I know how time consuming it can be at first. Try it out on a few smaller issues when you have time. This will teach your child the process and that you can be relied on not to flip out when he has a problem. Definitely use it when your child has more upsetting social conflicts…like the one below.

Sample Scenario 2

> DAUGHTER: (Crying.) I found out today that Meghan told her friends I am a slut.
> MOM: (Serious "Botox Brow" because you instantly want to kick Meghan.) Oh, no. I am so sorry. That's terrible! You have every right to be upset. How do you feel?
> DAUGHTER: Mad! She's such a liar! And she is the one who dates a ton of boys, not me. What is her problem?!
> MOM: I don't know. Do you want me to sit with you for a while? We can talk about it or just sit here.
> DAUGHTER: Yes. Just sit here.
> (Mom lets time pass until daughter talks.)
> DAUGHTER: I don't know what to do. I am so mad and I don't want to go to school tomorrow. Everyone's going to believe her.
> MOM: Resisting the urge to say any of the following:
> "No they won't believe her! You're such a nice girl."
> "Don't worry. I'll call her mom tonight and make sure she stops. And apologizes."

"But Meghan has always been a good friend. Could something be wrong with her?"

"Stay home tomorrow for a mental health day and you'll feel ready to face it the next day."

"Just stand up for yourself in front of everyone so they know you won't be treated that way."

"She's always been jealous of you."

Instead, say this:

Let's think of some ways you could handle this. I'll listen without judging at all and you can tell me any ideas you have.

DAUGHTER: I'd like to post on Instagram all the boys she's been out with this year so everyone knows who the real slut is.

MOM: Okay. That's one idea. What else could you do?

DAUGHTER: I could ask her why she said it.

MOM: Yeah. What else?

DAUGHTER: I could ask more people if they heard the same rumor.

MOM: Uh-huh. You could. Any other ideas?

DAUGHTER: I could tell the guidance counselor and have a meeting.

MOM: Yeah.

DAUGHTER: I don't know. I could write her a letter asking her to stop.

(Imagine this goes on for a while. Take your time, refrain from comment, gently encourage your daughter to think of more ideas; it's fine to sit in silence as your daughter thinks slowly.)

MOM: You are so good at solving problems. This is a great list. Do any of the ideas jump out at you? Which two do you like best?

DAUGHTER: The Instagram one and the one where I ask her why she said it.

MOM: (Refraining from shouting "The Instagram one?!?! Are you crazy? Can't you see how that will end?) Okay. What would happen if you posted that list on Instagram?

DAUGHTER: People would see what a hypocrite she is and not believe what she said about me.

MOM: Okay, so you put it up on Instagram and everyone sees it. Would anyone react badly?

DAUGHTER: Her friends would be mad. They would put something up about me.

MOM: Oh. That could be bad. Would you be okay with that?

DAUGHTER: No!

MOM: Sounds like it might start a war if you go that route. What about the other idea?

DAUGHTER: I could go up to her and ask her why she said it.

MOM: And how do you imagine her reacting?

DAUGHTER: If her friends are there she'll just lie and say she never said it.

MOM: Is there a chance you could talk with her alone?

DAUGHTER: Yeah, I could wait until after math class.

MOM: Okay, how do you think you'd say it?

DAUGHTER: Meghan, I heard you called me a slut and I want to know why?

MOM: All right. Did you actually hear her say it, or did someone else tell you?

DAUGHTER: (Light bulb!) Someone told me. Maybe I should ask her if she said it.

MOM: How would you do that?

DAUGHTER: I'd wait til she was alone and then say "Meghan, can we talk? I heard a rumor that you called me a slut and I just wanted to talk to you first about it."

MOM: Does that feel doable to you?

DAUGHTER: Yeah, I like that one to start with.

MOM: And would that help you feel less angry?

DAUGHTER: I think so.

MOM: Great. You're really good at thinking this through. Will you let me know how it goes?

THE END

When It Doesn't Go So Smoothly

That was pretty perfect, right? I know that in the real world it doesn't always go this smoothly. Sometimes your kid will be feeling extra impulsive (or extra vengeful) and things may not resolve as tidily as you'd hoped.

I've got some thoughts on handling those scenarios, but first, let's be clear on what kinds of solutions are truly out of the question. Anything that's illegal is easily a no-brainer. I would add anything that might result in disciplinary action from the school or another community organization would be a definite no. Finally, anything that would inflict severe emotional or physical damage on another person, or your own child, would also fall under the category of unacceptable.

How can you tell your kid that his solution is inappropriate without shutting him down completely? Let's start with the most cut and dry scenario in which his solution is illegal. Imagine a boy at school is teasing your son and your son's solution to the problem is to take the other kid's phone so he can't send humiliating texts anymore. Obviously stealing is illegal and you can't let your son trip down this path in the name of independent problem solving. You need to convey that his idea is a dead end without making your son feel like he's bad at problem solving. I would say something like this: "It would be tempting to do that, definitely. But... he'd probably just get another phone so I'm not sure that solves it. Plus, it's illegal to steal so I can't condone that or allow you to go in that direction. Let's keep thinking. Do you want to keep brainstorming or hear a couple ideas I had while you were talking?"

Sometimes, your kid won't go so far astray that she hits unlawful territory but she may be inclined toward the vengeful. In a scenario where a former friend betrays a tween girl, I can imagine her wanting to talk about it online in an attempt to rally people to her side. She may even be tempted to start a rumor or post embarrassing photos online to make the other girl look bad. If your kid suggests a solution that would inflict emotional or physical damage on someone else, or might provoke someone to inflict either on her, you can put your foot down just as you would if the proposed solution were illegal. Just remember to keep your language understanding and non-judgmental so you don't make your kid feel she's bad at solving problems. This is something she's learning and will need to practice before she's proficient. I might say something like, "I've seen people take that route before. It's really tempting but it never ends well. I can imagine in that scenario that one or both of you will get hurt beyond what's acceptable, so let's think through some other options. You're good at coming up with ideas. Do you want to keep listing ideas or do you want to hear a couple thoughts I had while you were talking?"

If you think the solution your kid proposes is vengeful but doesn't fall into the illegal or immoral category, remind her that the core of her problem isn't this other person, it's how this other person *made her feel*. She can't fix this other person, but she can fix how she herself feels. If she's feeling sad, lonely, disappointed, angry, or confused, ask if her solution really works toward fixing that emotion or if it is just a way to take action against someone else. Talk about how getting revenge can trick you into thinking you're doing the right thing because you're not being helpless, but it doesn't actually cure pain.

Another helpful strategy is asking your kid to pretend this problem belongs to someone else. Try casting a younger friend, sibling, or acquaintance into the same scenario and then brainstorming solutions for that child. This helps bring some perspective and neutrality to the scenario, plus the act of imagining a younger child in this role can bring out your own kid's protective instincts.

Finally, and perhaps most importantly, sometimes the best you can do is buy time. Middle schoolers are impulsive and the world of social media only compounds their desire for immediate reactions. If your child seems set on a bad choice, try saying something like this: "I promised I wouldn't judge you and I'm sticking by that. What I

ask from you is a promise that you won't do anything for 24 hours."
After a good night's sleep, your child may have a fresher perspective.
In the end, if you can slow her roll enough, she may see the benefits
of a less emotional response.

Once your child starts middle school, you will step down
as Chief Problem Solver and begin to play a support role as Problem Solving Trainer. It may feel counterintuitive, but you don't
need to be involved in solving your child's social conflicts unless
your child is suffering from ongoing emotional or physical threats.
In fact, your kid will become more resilient and competent if
she feels she can manage these herself with your support but not
interference.

> Social conflict often leaves a kid feeling helpless. This problem-
> solving process puts control back into your kid's hands so that
> she doesn't feel crippled by that loss of power.

This experience is all about teaching your child a process, not finding a silver-bullet solution. Don't worry if she lands on a solution that
seems too "soft" or too "bold." As she gets better at the process her
solutions will mature, too.

Letting kids solve their own problems can be highly uncomfortable for some parents. Do any of these concern you?

- Your kid isn't good at solving problems and you know she'll
  mess things up more trying to fix them.
- Your kid won't do anything to solve the problem unless you
  do. He'll just ignore it.
- You should be teaching your kid the right thing to do, not letting him flounder.
- You like feeling needed and you want to help. It's no fun not
  being needed by your middle schooler.

- With all of your experience, you're sure you know the right answer, if only he would listen.

I understand why all of these would tug at you during this time in your child's development. They're all valid statements. Let's look at them critically to see how they hold up.

Your kid isn't good at solving problems and you know she'll mess things up more by trying to fix them. In middle school, it may be accurate that your kid isn't good at solving problems. But becoming good at problem solving isn't something that happens when you hit a certain age. It happens when you practice. At first, she will be bad. But if you start now letting her try, by high school she'll be experienced and able to handle the trickier problems that come with getting older. On the flip side, if you don't start now, you lose the opportunity to embed these skills into her brain during the formative years. Practice solving problems, and practice often, to cement this critical skill into your child's developing brain.

Your kid won't do anything to solve the problem unless you do. He'll just ignore it. Believe me, I get it. My son would much rather let things evolve naturally than put time and effort into shaping their outcome. His philosophy is "things usually just work themselves out." As a more proactive, slightly type A kind of mom, this frustrates me. But you know what, he's right. More power to him if he doesn't stress out over the small stuff. Don't solve problems for your kid that he's willing to let go. It's not your problem, and if it's not bothering him, it's not his problem either.

You should be teaching your kid the right thing to do, not letting him flounder. As strange as it may seem, these two sentiments are not mutually exclusive. By hand delivering solutions to your kid every time he has a problem, you're not doing him any favors in the long run. Floundering is how he figures out what works best for him, and he then becomes a more resilient and self-reliant young adult.

You like feeling needed and you want to help. It's no fun not being needed by your middle schooler. Turning over the reins of problem solving in no way means your child doesn't need you anymore. There are lots of ways you can provide comfort and support to your child without stifling her development. In fact, as an active and nonjudgmental listener, you become even more valuable to your tween through the middle school years. You'll be surprised how much more often your child approaches you with her problems once you stop trying to solve them.

With all of your experience, you know you have the right answer (and you can quickly spot the wrong ones), if only he would listen. It's important that your child come up with his own solution, one that he believes will work best for him based on his personality, his situation, and the other people involved. Only your son knows all of these details and only he can assess his comfort level with the solution that suits him best.

Whatever problems or situations your kid encounters in middle school, following these steps will help her develop social management skills that will benefit her through the tween years and beyond. While her initial reaction will be emotional, these steps allow her to be practical and methodical (something that is just not natural for most adolescents). When your kid solves her own problem, she practices important skills so they become automatic. She then implements the solution more confidently and gains self-esteem when the situation is resolved. Self-esteem can't be given out as easily as a participation trophy. It must be earned through success at overcoming challenges, like solving your own problems.

THE PROBLEM-SOLVING PATH™

1. Listen with a neutral face while your kid talks about the problem.

2. Ask him how the problem makes him feel.

3. Ask him to come up with a list of ways he could solve his problem. Promise not to react negatively to any of his ideas.

4. Ask him to pick his favorite two solutions, then to imagine out loud and step-by-step how each would play out in real life.

5. Double check. Would that outcome make you feel less _____?

6. Let him pick the one with the best outcome for him.

7. Tell him you're happy to listen anytime and that you hope he'll let you know how it goes.

Problem–Solving Flow Chart

PART 2

Helping Your Kid Through Real Middle School Problems

I hope you now have a greater appreciation for your middle schooler's developing brain, quest for an independent identity, unique communication needs, and ability to solve her own problems. As parents we can either fight against these universal changes or accept them. In the best-case scenario, we embrace and celebrate the changes our kids are going through. This is the foundation for being a happier parent, and having a happier kid, through the tricky middle school years.

What follows are the thirteen scenarios that parents ask me about most frequently. They are common middle school social dilemmas happening all over America—and maybe even in your own house— that cause parents and kids to get all kinds of flustered. Building on the theories of adolescent development and parenting I cover in part 1, we'll dive deeper into what's really happening in middle school and, through easy-to-follow, practical advice, get you *unflustered* in no time.

Note: If you've turned right to this section to find help with a problem, you should know that the most common complaint I hear is "My kid won't tell me anything." You won't find that scenario in this section because it gets its very own chapter. Flip to chapter 4 if that's your primary concern. Otherwise, onward!

#1

"Everyone Has an Instagram but Me"

Coming to Terms with Your Child's Entry into the New World of Social Media

My sixth-grade daughter wants an Instagram account. I know *"everyone's got one,"* but what about mean girls, stalkers, and topless Miley Cyrus photos? She might think she's ready, but I'm not.

Social media is a part of our kids' lives, like it or not, so it's futile trying to keep them away from it entirely. Lots of kids who are prohibited from opening an account get sneaky and open a private account under a fake name. Others just go on friends' accounts to see all the stuff you're keeping them from. You may be thinking, "Yeah, and drinking is still gonna happen in middle school but that doesn't mean I am going to buy my eighth grader beer." True. And social media does have a dark side just like underage drinking. But the analogy dies right there because, unlike underage drinking, social media use among middle schoolers can have quite a few big upsides...if you're willing to be a part of it.

Personally, I like social media and use it to my advantage. Through Instagram, I can keep up with my kids' ever-changing interests, hobbies, passions, and friends. They're changing quickly, and Instagram gives me clues as to ways I can steer conversations so our talk is relevant to them.

Equally as important, social media gives me a peek at the sad stuff going on in my kids' and their friends' lives. Last year, a girl at my daughter's school attempted suicide. When she found out, my daughter went back to the girl's Instagram account and showed me her posts from days before the attempt. We noticed several that looked like cries for help. It was a good way for us to talk about the sometimes overwhelming emotions of being thirteen and better ways to handle them. Now I keep an eye out for posts that signal a kid may need extra support. If I see something, I may offer an encouraging compliment or talk with my own kids about being sensitive. In the event that things looked really bad, I could go further. Yes, the things we see in our kids' social media world may be upsetting. We may get offended by some of it. But, as NBC taught me as a kid, "The more you know, the more you grow." Social media can be a great peephole into our kids' inner thoughts if we are brave enough to take a look. Rather than throw out social media altogether, I integrate it into our family lifestyle so I can mitigate the risks by keeping an eye on it and use the positives to our advantage.

Social media changes quickly. Whether your kids are on Instagram or another of the latest, greatest platforms that keeps popping up, the philosophy and guidelines below will help you wade through the social media waters with purpose and pleasure. For the purpose of continuity, I'll use Instagram as the platform of choice for this section.

Most parents I know lump Instagram into one of these categories:

1. Pointless social media app that lets kids share pictures. Big deal.
2. Growling social monster that eats up our kids' self-esteem, making them uncharacteristically mean, weak for approval, pathetically brand conscious, and limp with self-pity.

I offer an alternative view:

3. Creative communication tool that kids use to express their interests and concerns, and powerful parenting tool that lets us stay connected with kids when they begin to pull away during the tween years.

Are you slightly more interested now? I hope so, because Instagram has a lot to offer. That's not to say there aren't important ways to be cautious. As you would before you put any tool into your child's hands, you must teach him how to use it safely and productively. But before we get into the *how* of Instagram, I'll make a case for the *why*.

When kids become tweens, they begin the important job of developing an identity apart from their parents. Naturally, this involves spending more time alone or with peers and less time tucked under your parental wing. This can be sad for you, and you may wonder how to stay close during this period of change. Social media is a great way to witness your child's developing values, humor, relationships, interests, and concerns. It gives you the opportunity to talk about things that truly interest your kid. Perhaps you notice on your daughter's account several posts of hockey pictures. You never knew she even liked hockey! Maybe she has found a genuine new interest, or maybe the cute boy in fourth block plays hockey and she's quick to seem a fan. Either way, seeing a new trend allows you to open up casual conversations that could lead to bigger topics.

Some of you are thinking, fine, it's one thing to see pictures of hockey, or horses, or even a shirtless Liam Hemsworth, but I'm concerned about the far less innocent things my kid might see—or post—online. What kinds of things are we talking about? Beauty contests in which kids rank one another based on appearance. SpongeBob dropping the f-bomb. A middle school couple kissing. (Honestly, this is one of the grosser things you could ever see. They look like children, and I can only imagine the noxious smell of Skittles and Axe body spray colliding. Barf.) A cartoon marijuana leaf. Kids trying out sexy poses. An expression of self-hatred.

I understand that you don't want your kid to see any of these things. But it is a fact that, even without an Instagram account, your kid will *still* see these images on a friend's phone or tablet.

> If your child doesn't have an account that you monitor, you will not see the photos she sees. Because you will not see them, you will miss the opportunity to talk about them with your child, leaving her to process the experience alone or through the comments of her peers.

So, how do you help your child use social media safely while still having fun? That is, after all, the point of it all. Here are my Instagram (and general social media) Guidelines for you and your child:

1. Before you give your kid access to any new technology, let her know you must have her password, and you can browse through the content at any time.

2. Set the expectation that you will review your child's use...less and less as she exhibits proper online behavior. Yes, that means you can and should read her texts, posts, and other technical and public forms of communication. Do not read her diary or journal.

3. Set expectations for proper etiquette and safety online. If boundaries are crossed you can address them without your child being shocked because you've already established your limits. For example, at my house, the list includes: no using your last name on social media accounts, no posting pictures of your school, no name-calling, no allowing your phone to post your location, no swearing, no embarrassing someone else (siblings included!), and no spamming your followers with too many posts.

4. Start a conversation by talking about something positive you saw on her account. Later that evening, start with "I love the picture you posted of the kitten hangin' in there 'til Friday. That was so cute! Did you edit that?"

5. Push only if a casual attempt fails. "Hey, I know this is uncomfortable but your ticket to using your device and being allowed on that platform is talking to me about things like this. I won't do it often, but occasionally if something is offensive, we need to talk about it to be sure you understand. That's my job. Here is what I found troublesome about that picture..."

6. Promise to never post negative or corrective comments on your kid's posts, or her friend's posts, online. If something catches your attention and warrants a conversation, promise you will have it privately.

7. Most importantly, promise you will have this conversation calmly and rationally. The moment you flip out because you saw something inappropriate on Instagram is the moment your kid resolves never to tell you anything important again. Quite possibly, this is followed by the moment he creates a new Instagram account under a disguised name.

8. Wait a while to bring up errors in judgment. If you see something that concerns you related to ethics, morality, or manners, wait until later that evening or the next day to say something. Don't comment on what shocks you as you look over your child's shoulder. She'll turn off her device and shut down the conversation immediately. If you have a safety concern, address that right away.

9. Bring up an offending item casually using exploratory questions. "Did you see that picture of the guy grabbing the girl's chest? I couldn't tell if the girl was embarrassed, could you?"

10. Don't intervene often. Truly, this is your kid's new playground and he won't want you hovering there constantly.

Save the comments for serious issues of safety or morality and let the rest of it slide. He's just trying to figure things out so, whenever possible, default to cutting him some slack.

11. Ask your child what level of positive interaction is acceptable to him. Is it okay to compliment him on a picture? What about his friends? Let him tell you what's acceptable and what's embarrassing. In my opinion, less is more when it comes to interacting with your kids on social media. You want to say enough so people know you're there, but you're not trying to be the life of the party.

12. Be sure any geotagging/mapping feature is turned off. This means pictures your kid posts will not identify her location.

13. Do not allow your kid to post any photos with your home address or activity locations obviously displayed.

14. When naming his account, tell your child to use his first and middle name only, or a nickname (SoccerStar2000) but not his last name.

15. Have a conversation with your kid about collecting "likes." Some kids use Instagram as a way to campaign for popularity. They enter "beauty contests" or beg for more "likes" on their posts. Ask questions that encourage critical thinking like, "Why would a girl want to be evaluated on her beauty by a bunch of people she doesn't know?"; "How do you think the lowest-ranked girls feel?"; "What would happen if you and a friend posted the same picture but hers got more likes?"

16. Encourage your kid to devote an Instagram account to a hobby or theme she loves. My daughter, for example, loves Harry Potter and The Hunger Games, so she has an Instagram account devoted to the books and films. No one even knows she manages the account, and one of the actresses in the newest Hunger Games movie gave her a compliment on Instagram, which made her ~~day~~, ~~week~~, LIFE. Her experience

is not about collecting likes from peers; it's about celebrating her favorite stories with fans who feel the same way. Full disclosure: she has a personal account, too, so we've covered all of the points above.

17. Encourage creativity. There are lots of apps your kid can download to make edits. Rather than just posting "selfies" (a picture she takes of herself, often with a weird duck-faced expression) or reposting what others have made, your kid can become an experienced young graphic designer, selecting images, quotes, and treatments to convey her personal style.

18. Teach your child how to create a well-rounded social media identity. Your involvement can't begin and end with you telling him everything he's not allowed to do. Inspire him with ways he can create a complete picture of himself online. See my infographic for creating a more well-rounded online image.

19. Know that even if your kid rolls her eyes, she still hears you.

Should you allow all social media? *No!* My least favorite app right now is ask.fm. It's a popular site where kids post polling questions with the option to answer anonymously. Because of this, it often turns vicious and/or sexually perverse quickly. Avoid this one at all costs.

Teach your kid to use social media well and to present a more well-rounded online image with these graphics.

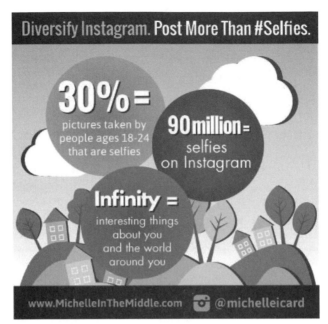

Diversify Instagram. Post More Than #Selfies.

30% = pictures taken by people ages 18-24 that are selfies

90 million = selfies on Instagram

Infinity = interesting things about you and the world around you

www.MichelleInTheMiddle.com 📷 @michelleicard

Instafun #1

FORMULA FOR INSTAGRAM FUN

10%	Having Fun with Friends
10%	Hobbies or Special Interests
10%	Food
10%	Pets & Family
10%	Inspirational Messages
10%	Sharing or Asking for Information
10%	Personal Causes You Support
10%	Humorous
10%	Pics of You That Aren't Selfies
10%	Selfies

www.MichelleInTheMiddle.com 📷 @michelleicard

Instafun #2 Concerned about narcissism? Show kids how to use social media well.

#2

Goodbye, Birds and Bees—Hello, Porn

Answering Your Middle Schooler's
More Advanced Questions About Sex

My sixth-grade son came home and asked, "Hey Mom, what is sixty-nine?" I screamed, "Oh my God! It's the number after sixty-eight, now go do your homework!" Do I really have to explain this to him? I'd rather die.

I've been presented with variations on this scenario by many parents who are dying inside at these kinds of questions and don't know what to do. While that is a completely normal reaction, please don't let sexual questions shut you down completely. Truly, the fact that your son trusts you enough to ask means you've done something right thus far. Chin up and stay strong. You can do this.

Because your son is only in sixth grade, your instinct may be to put him off. "You're too young to know about things like that" or "I'm not comfortable telling you" are not acceptable responses. He's obviously embarrassed and wouldn't ask you for the fun of it. Not knowing causes him enough anxiety that he needs an answer, and if it doesn't come from you, it's coming from Google.

Let's pause on that for a second. Recently, a mom shared a story with me about looking through her computer's search history, only to find links to a pornographic video clip. When she asked her daughter what that was about, the girl dissolved into tears. "Everyone at school was talking about 'fisting' and I was the only one who didn't know what it meant. I just wanted to know what it meant." What upset the little girl far more than being in trouble was what she had seen on the computer. "Is that how adults treat each other?" she cried.

I'm sad at that piece of innocence lost and even more heartbroken at the misinterpretation of what this girl must have seen on that video as normal adult behavior. These days, answers to their every question lay at your kids' fingertips. When kids come to you with questions, you don't have to tell them everything. You should, though, give them enough of an answer to keep their curiosity from driving them to research more on their own.

By the time a kid is in middle school, he will be exposed to just about every sexual innuendo, joke, and slang term you can imagine (and many that you cannot). It's not just Google with the answers, either. The kids on the bus, in gym class, and at the lunch table are quick to seem experts. And when no one really knows, one kid who feigns intelligence can quickly become the cafeteria Dr. Ruth. If you want your child to have accurate information about human sexuality and development, it needs to come from you or another trusted adult.

Conversations about sex are among the hardest for parents to have with middle schoolers. Once kids head to middle school, they suddenly hear all kinds of things and are eager to seem like experts among friends. Start identifying yourself as the knowledge manager in your family early on. When your kid sees that you don't overreact when she asks these "shocking" questions, she'll also learn she can come to you about any of the other hot topics for this age, including: drugs, bullying, body image, and relationship abuse, and you will be there for her.

If you find yourself in this uncomfortable situation, here is what you can do:

1. Take a deep (yet undramatic) breath.

2. Admit that it's hard to talk about these things, but tell your son you're glad he came to you to ask so you can give him accurate information.

3. Say enough to squelch curiosity. "Sixty-nine is a nickname for a sexual position involving two adults." Maybe that's enough. It's likely he doesn't want to know more, he just needs minimal information to save face among his peers in case this comes up again.

4. Answer follow-up questions. If he wants to know more, you have to give accurate answers. In this case, it would involve a brief definition of oral sex. I suggest you consult a good sex ed book for the right language. It's okay to say to your kid, "Give me some time to think about this so I can be sure I'm explaining it right. I'll tell you tomorrow."

5. Use the opportunity to work values into the conversation, as in, two people who decide to have a sexual relationship should always respect each other and listen to the other person. Any choice during sex should be made based on feeling love and pleasure, never pressure.

6. Ask your own questions: "How have you heard people use that word?" or "Is that what you wanted to know?"

7. Reassure him that you're glad he asked. Say something like, "I know it's strange to talk about this stuff, but I'm glad you came to me. You can always ask me about stuff like this."

8. Provide appropriate resources to answer any questions you're not comfortable addressing yourself. This can be a close friend, a pediatrician, or a good book. You don't have to be the expert at everything; you just need to know where to go for help.

#3

Good Girls Gone Bad

Helping When Girls Turn Against Each Other

My daughter was part of a group of girls last year, but this year they have abandoned her. There seems to be a ringleader in the group telling the other girls to stay away from my daughter. I'm heartbroken and angry. What do I do?

Sadly, this is one of the more common social scenarios in middle school. Having been there myself as a kid, I know how raw this can be for both child and parent to experience. Although this is purely educational and not intended to ease your pain, it may be useful to remember what's happening to your daughter and her peers at this stage of their brain development. If you find it annoying to give them a little grace, I understand. Nevertheless, here's more background on the changing tides of middle school friendships.

During middle school (and most commonly in seventh grade) kids start to freak out a little bit about who they are in relationship to their peers. It's their primary goal to develop an identity apart from family, so that one day they can successfully leave your house and have a job, apartment, and relationships of their own.

Figuring out who they are requires determining where they fit in the social pyramid being constructed by their peers. This is difficult for both boys and girls, but pop culture has done a special disservice to tween girls. A quick scan of my local bookstore shelves recently enlightened me on this. Books aimed at girls age twelve to fifteen are hitting a level of sexuality and adult themes that I found shocking. But beyond that, there was something more subtle and insidious happening. Books for teen girls today still capitalize on the number one fear of adolescents, not being normal, but the big difference is that today's reads put way too much emphasis on being *perfect*. Is perfect the new normal? Boy, are we in trouble. This causes some girls to go on the offensive to be sure they're not the one who will be left out. Psychologists call this "relational aggression," in which one girl seeks to hurt another by damaging her relationship with her peers, often through gossip or public humiliation. Because the media tells girls so often that they need to be perfect, girls will draw attention to one another's flaws and hide their own at all costs, creating a culture of social aggression.

In addition to cultural pressure to be more *normal* (more *perfect*), girls go through natural and expected friendship changes when they get to middle school. Interests change, they make new friends, they perceive themselves as a different level of "cool" than old friends, and sometimes they don't have the vocabulary or manners to know how to deal with this. While friendships coming to an end in middle school is a perfectly normal thing, that doesn't make it hurt less. Our girls need to be taught how to talk through these changes without victimizing one another.

Like I said, this probably doesn't make you feel better about your daughter's situation, but it does explain why middle school girls can get a reputation for being mean. I dislike this blanket statement. It's along the same lines as "Female managers can be so bitchy." The problem isn't that middle school girls are mean (though I'll admit that *some* of them are horrible). Generally speaking, the problem is that they're a hot mess of emotions and they feel completely helpless...so they often misstep.

If you find yourself parenting a child in this situation, here are some things you can do:

1. Empathize with your daughter first and foremost: "That is awful. I went through something similar"—or—"I had a friend who went through something similar. I know how hard it is and I'm so sorry."

2. Don't go overboard. Asking too many questions, making it the dinner conversation every night, taking it personally, demanding that your daughter/the teacher/other parents/other kids take certain actions is ludicrous. Remain detached. Your daughter will (eventually) thank you for it.

3. Give your daughter some power by going through the problem-solving process outlined in chapter 5. A social blindside would make anyone feel helpless. Let her preserve some power and dignity by choosing a response that suits her. And if at first she doesn't succeed, encourage her to try again.

4. Spend extra effort making your daughter's life a bit more comfortable. Invite new friends to the movies and pay for them. Take her for ice cream. Keep her active. Distraction is a powerful tool. Along these lines, afford a little extra grace if your daughter snaps at you more than usual.

5. Don't bash the other girls. Your daughter will take this as a personal attack against her judgment when choosing friends. Also, more times than not, I've seen girls come back together and your daughter won't be able to forget what you said. She may feel she has to sneak around with her friend to avoid your criticism.

6. Gently remind your daughter not to burn bridges. The tides of tween friendships change quickly and dramatically. If your daughter can rise above gossip she will be rewarded when other girls (and boys) see her resistance to drama and take her

side. "Kill 'em with kindness" is a great motto. I'm not saying you should encourage your child to be a doormat. I'm saying teach her not to stoop to someone else's level.

7. Take stronger action if the situation becomes worse over time. Your daughter may need to talk with a professional counselor to get coping tips during this time. It helps. Sometimes switching classes, or even schools, is a good idea, too. I would not do these without some social coaching as well. You're only hearing half of a story, after all. Your daughter (knowingly or not) may have contributed to the problem, and talking with a counselor may help her identify areas she can work on socially.

8. Encourage her to seek out new friends, to not force herself into the old friendships. There are too many good people in the world to worry about being friends with the others.

One final piece of advice: before this ever happens, encourage your kids to keep their friendship eggs in different baskets. What do I mean by this? You've probably heard the saying "Don't keep all your eggs in one basket." Imagine me, on a bike, riding down a peaceful road on a lovely day with a basket of farm-fresh eggs on the front of my bike. The sun is shining and I am whistling. Suddenly, a rock in the middle of the path catches my wheel and with a twist I'm thrown from the bike as it crashes in the path, covering me in dust and raw egg yolks!

Friendships, like eggs, are fragile. Limiting yourself to one set of friends is like keeping all your eggs in one basket. If your friends are all in the same clique, when any one of you hits a bump in the road you *all* get covered in the mess. Help your daughter stay in touch with friends from elementary school, make time for neighborhood friends, connect with people on sports teams, and, most importantly, encourage her to branch out at a new school to make friends from different social groups. This will ensure that she has more places to go when things get bumpy or messy.

#4

There's More Than One Way to Be Cool

*Helping Your Son Make Connections with
Other Guys When He Doesn't Play Sports*

**My son is such a good guy, but he doesn't play, or even
have much interest in, sports. He has a hard time getting
to know other boys without the natural sports connection.
How can I help him fit in better with his peers?**

I hear it often from parents of middle school boys: *"It would be so much
easier for my son if he could play sports."*

True. Playing sports is a rite of passage for many boys, and the
lessons, camaraderie, and thrills brought by being part of a team
are priceless. But we do boys a disservice when we glorify sports as
the be-all and end-all of popularity. There are lots of ways boys can
develop social collateral that they can trade in for cool points. Here
are just some.

1. Learn to play an instrument. Strike that—a *cool* instrument.
   Strike that again. Learn to play *cool music* on any instrument.
   We all know that for tween boys, there are no instruments
   cooler than guitar or drums. Those would be my first two
   choices for helping a kid earn street cred. But if your boy
   insists that trombone is his passion, buy him some culturally
   relevant sheet music. Remember when Casey Abrams played

stand-up bass on *American Idol?* That kid could have easily gone in a different direction, but he pulled off cool by playing hot music with swagger. The unexpected instrument actually added to his mystique.

2. Make and manage money. Is this any different from our societal expectations of cool adult men? Boys who know how to make money and how to manage it (i.e., not being overly flashy or trying to buy friendships but being chill enough to spring for a pizza after school) come across as competent leaders. Encourage your son's earning power by helping him start a small business, teach him to do manual labor over the summer, explain investment, and begin to develop his reliable and hardworking persona.

3. Be funny. What is it about a funny guy that's just so cool? A good sense of humor demands bravery, intelligence, confidence, and a dash of empathy. My husband recently paused a hidden camera show we watch as a family to explain to our kids that the reason the pranks are funny is that no one is being humiliated or teased for the laugh. This is an important point to make with tweens and teens when flexing the good humor muscle.

4. Talk sports. Your son may not be particularly good at playing sports, but he should understand the vocabulary of athletes. Think Jonah Hill as Peter Brand in *Moneyball.* We only really play team sports for a short time in our lives. As adults, it's the language of sports that matters most.

5. Know how to fix things. Show your son how to change the oil in your car, repair a flat bike tire, pump gas, replace windshield wipers, use sharp cooking knives to butcher meat, or perform CPR. Working with his hands is an impressive way to build social collateral...and as your boy becomes a teen, car maintenance and repair become really cool.

6. Develop strong body language. It's not that we always notice when boys do this well, but a *lack* of strong body language can be glaring and spotlight a boy as a social target. Make sure your boy makes eye contact, shakes hands firmly, holds the door, and stands tall. Start young.

7. Be active outside of team sports. Explore unexpected ways your son might get his body moving. Break dancing, yoga, hiking, archery, rock climbing... anything to help your boy learn how to enjoy being a physical person.

8. Be "the man" at one thing. I bet we all know someone who earned peer approval for being the best at something notoriously dorky. In my high school there was a boy so into student government he carried a briefcase instead of a backpack. At first the kids balked and teased, but he was relentless in his love for politics and eventually the class rallied around him. Help your son find his thing and do everything you can to support him as he leans into that obsession. He can enter competitions, win some ribbons, and earn some hardware to show that he's the best. Winning is definitely a valuable social currency and a self-confidence booster, which is also very cool.

Beyond the things listed above that your son can do to feel cooler, here are some things *you* can do if he is struggling socially:

1. Notice what your son enjoys doing most of all and encourage a deeper pursuit. Many of you are thinking, "But for my son it's video games and I'm not supposed to encourage that." Not true. If your son loves video games more than anything in the world, this may parlay into a passion for graphic design, app development, CGI, filmmaking, or real-life war reenactments (to name a handful).

2. Don't transfer your own needs to your son. Some kids don't need a lot of friends. They may be introverts or just the quiet type, and there's nothing wrong with that. If his lifestyle is personally satisfying, don't worry just because *you* would need more social interaction to be happy.

3. Spend a little time or money if your son is worried about not being cool. You don't have to buy all name-brand clothes, but if a certain brand of sneakers would help, make the investment. If allowing a sleepover and having the right snacks would help (I'm not talking grapes and granola bars—I'm talking ice cream sundaes or chugging soda right out of the two liter), then occasionally take one for your son's team and be the cool house. Remember, at this age he's exploring how he fits into his peer environment. If he asks for help, make it easier on him.

One final thought. When I ask adults who have visited their high school reunions about the graduates who ended up being the most successful, rarely is it the most popular jock. While there's nothing wrong with sports being your passion, playing that sport shouldn't define who you are as a person, because it has a very limited life span. That's hard for a twelve-year-old boy to internalize.

I named my boys' leadership program Hero's Pursuit based on the work of Joseph Campbell, the philosopher, writer, and mythologist who famously coined the phrase "Follow your bliss." Campbell wrote about universal truths pervasive in all cultures and all times. One of the most interesting to me is the need for a boy to feel heroic. To be heroic, in fact, is what it takes in every culture for a boy to become a man.

How does a middle school boy fulfill his primal need to be a hero? To do this, a boy must experience a "quest," or a time when he leaves the comfort of his group, undertakes a challenge, and then returns triumphant.

I know this sounds very Dungeons & Dragons, but it's not so much sci-fi as the reality of our human condition. It seems like these days, boys are suffering from a loss of rituals around growing up. Middle-class kids largely get what they want, when they want it. Sure, lots of parents employ incentive charts to reward good behavior or teach discipline and self-control, but I'm talking about a real challenge and reward, not just the passing of days. Our boys need to be challenged to feel satisfied.

> In my program Hero's Pursuit, guys learn that a hero's quest is to do something brave for the benefit of his community. An act of bravery can be a physical feat or the delivery of a life-changing message.

Quests can come in many forms. We, as parents, need to recognize and ritualize them as much as possible. Hiking the Appalachian Trail, standing up to a bully, starting an organization, delivering a speech, or volunteering at a homeless shelter are all types of personal quests boys can undertake.

As parents, we should encourage our sons to think and act independently. If it is a quest your son needs to grow into a man, then consider the many ways you can make that possible by opening up new and extraordinary opportunities for him.

#5
Put-Downs and Comebacks

Preparing to Deal with the Middle School Bully

My daughter is being bullied at school. Do I make her stick up for herself, change schools, let her stay home? I'm at a loss. How do I help her get through this?

To begin with, I'm sorry she's going through this. This is becoming an increasingly common topic, but that doesn't make it any less painful when your child is targeted. It can feel like your heart is being stepped on to discover that someone you love is being systematically excluded, harassed, or humiliated for another person's social gain.

Because bullying is so devastating, I want to be sure we're working from the same definition, because the response to bullying should be swift and strong.

For the purposes of this section and the work I do with middle schoolers, I define bullying as someone repeatedly using his power (social or physical) to degrade, harass, or humiliate someone else.

Bullying has become such a hot topic in our society that it's now a blanket term people use whenever someone is a jerk. We shouldn't teach our children that every time someone mistreats them they have been bullied. Incorrectly using the term "bully" over-victimizes people who aren't being bullied and underrepresents what a bullying victim goes through.

Before you read on, spend a minute thinking about whether

your child is being bullied. I'm not asking you to do this to downgrade your child's bad experience. I only want you to have a clear definition so you can take the best action in response to your child's situation.

Bullying *is* a problem, but we can't solve it if we mislabel everything offensive as bullying. A one-time remark can be offensive, hurtful, or embarrassing. Bullying is bigger than that even. The scars of being repeatedly victimized last much longer. Kids and adults need to understand the difference so that we can effectively help kids respond to both situations.

I've heard parents say their daughter was bullied when a friend decided not to invite her to a sleepover. They thought that since their daughter had been invited in the past, expected to be invited, and had been friends with the larger group of girls going to the sleepover, her exclusion was humiliating and distressing enough to qualify as bullying. In their rush to defend their daughter's right to be included, they mislabeled her experience and branded her a victim.

Things get a little muddy when one person becomes the target of an entire community. It may be that on any given day Sarah is teased by Caroline in math, tripped by Natalie in the hall, told she cannot sit at a half-full table by Margaret at lunch, and is the subject of Shana's nasty text after school. Is Sarah being bullied even though none of these girls repeatedly targeted her? Of course. From Sarah's perspective, she still feels the steady stream of abuse, perhaps even more so because she has been deemed an outsider by a larger group, leaving her with nowhere to escape. In cases like this, the school needs to make some cultural changes to build more empathy, lower tolerance for acts of rudeness, and raise student awareness about the domino effect from this kind of behavior. A character or social leadership program implemented by caring and respected teachers goes a long way here. For more on the social leadership program I wrote, please visit my website, MichelleintheMiddle.com.

Assuming your child is being bullied, here are some things you can do:

1. **Use the problem-solving process in chapter 5 to give your child back some power.** Whether your kid is a target of repeated bullying or has to deal with the occasional rude comments or actions of a peer, she may feel helpless. Let her brainstorm a response she feels most comfortable with to restore some of her personal power.

2. **Alert teachers and support staff at school about the bullying.** Follow up with regular meetings to ensure your child is safe and that conditions are improving. Your child does not need to know you're doing this. You can decide if telling your kid will make him feel embarrassed or encouraged by your support. Regardless, you should still be talking directly with the school.

3. **Do not call the parents of the bullies.** This never works. You will simply drag in more opinions to cloud the issue. Resist the urge to avenge your kid by punishing the bully. It may sound like that would be satisfying and fair, but it never ends well. Let karma do this job for you.

4. **Don't over-victimize your kid.** Don't let your daughter hear you talking with other adults about her being bullied. That only furthers her humiliation. This is a personal matter, not to be shared with your peers, unless it is done privately. Complaining or crying out loud only adds the burden of your reaction to your daughter's experience.

5. **Take the situation seriously.** Bullying can have devastating and long-term effects. If you find out your child is being bullied, offer empathy and clearly express that you're on your child's side.

6. **Find a qualified adult to counsel your child.** A guidance counselor may or may not be a good fit, as she may have an obligation to all the kids involved. An outside therapist is

removed from the situation and can be 100 percent on your child's side. Look for a counselor who will give your kid tools in addition to talk.

7. **Get creative when it comes to nurturing friendships.** It's amazing how resilient people can be in the face of exclusion. Often, one good friend is all it takes to carry us through tough times. Find ways to forge a connection for your child with a peer. If your kid isn't connecting with anyone at school or through activities, get even more creative. Have a cousin come spend the summer at your house, try overnight camp, or find a special program/social skills group for kids who've been bullied. If the situation persists, your child may need to switch schools. That's okay, too. It can be helpful for your child to start over or reinvent himself or his reputation.

8. **Nurture a hobby as a source of joy.** Make sure your child has a recurring time and place to have social fun. Whatever she loves doing, be that video games or babysitting, encourage her to take classes or join groups where she can be with others who share that idea of fun.

9. **Find a place for your kid to participate in a character education or social leadership program.** Find one you like and recommend it to your school, scout troop, summer camp, or youth group. The more places kids can practice problem solving and experience one another's perspectives, the less pervasive bullying will be.

It's a tall order, so I don't recommend this lightly, but staying unflustered even in the face of your kid's personal crisis will model a positive reaction, keep her from feeling more self-doubt, and unburden her from the pressure of carrying both of you through this. With your steady support she'll begin to feel stronger and more capable of handling aggressors. As you see her doing this, you'll begin to feel some relief, too, knowing that she can take care of herself.

#6

Not My Kid—Oh, Wait . . .

*Discovering Your Kid Has Been a Bully, or
Maybe Just a Jerk, or Probably Just Human*

**I've been commiserating with a friend about a string of
mean texts her son received from some boys at school.
Much to my embarrassment and anger, I've now discovered
that my son was one of those boys. What do I do?**

Oh, boy, this is a tough one. As in the last scenario, it's important to
correctly identify the behavior. Before you label your son a bully (or
let anyone else label him that way), try to determine whether this is
a one-time deal or if he's repeatedly hurting a target. Regardless of
what you call it, you certainly want to help your son put a fast end to
his hurtful behavior.

First, talk with your son to see what he says about the situation.
He might be relieved to come clean. He might offer some kind of
justification, like, "That kid is so mean! He acts like he has the perfect family and he makes fun of our family!" When confronted, you
see that he feels emotional and conflicted about the drama. To me,
a kid who has a strong emotional response to an accusation of bullying is not in as much danger as one who downplays it. His behavior probably comes from a place of insecurity, anger, and doubt. He
would benefit from emotional support and one-on-one counseling
with a therapist to learn how to resolve his anger without verbally

or physically hurting someone else. In this case, you would know at least that your son was acting out because he sensed an injustice, not out of a desire to be mean, manipulative, or cruel.

If your kid has a less emotional response to being accused of bullying, you should be more concerned. A child who denies wrongdoing, or acts shocked at having been misinterpreted or misunderstood, sounds like a bully to me. Did someone call Eddie Haskell? To sweep his bad actions under the carpet, he'll quickly offer to apologize to his target so you'll think of him as perfect again. He might say, "Oh, wow! I had no idea Grant was so sensitive. Seriously, he takes things way too personally. I'll just apologize tomorrow." This kind of response disregards another kid's reactions, blames others for lacking a "sense of humor," and suggests that an apology will fix everything. This type of response will require more effort to correct and much closer observation.

One of the things you should be doing is looking closely at his online communication. Presumably, you own all the technology your kid uses. Even if you didn't pay for his iPad, you should still regulate use of all technology in your home. You should perform regular spot checks on his device (phone, tablet, etc.) to make sure he is using it appropriately. Evidence may have been deleted, but if you do see something alarming you are within proper parenting bounds to question it.

Middle schoolers are human, too. All of us mess up at one time or another, in middle school especially. Some of us laughed when another kid was teased, or we didn't stick up for the kid who looked uncomfortable. Others made a calculated decision to exclude someone for being different. Some of us were more proactive, hitting, spreading rumors, or coming up with the horrible nickname that stuck. We have to afford all kids some grace during the middle school years. Part of figuring out a new identity is trying on all kinds of social positions and social tools for size. This is a messy business and mistakes will be made. Offering forgiveness and understanding when your child makes a mistake, even one that hurts another child, is a good way to model better behavior.

Regardless of whether you have evidence, when you hear that your child is a bully or simply that your child did something to hurt another child, here are some things you can do:

1. Ask your child for his side of the story and evaluate his response without emotion.
2. Set expectations for the respectful treatment of others, especially those who seem different, more sensitive, or weaker than others.
3. Accept that even the best child—yes, your child—is capable of hurting other people, even repeatedly, but that this does not define your child's character going forward.
4. Model forgiveness and reinforce that you support and love your child despite the mistake(s) she made.
5. Don't investigate for evidence through other families. This is no one else's business. If evidence is in your home, or is delivered to you, that's fine. But don't go digging. You only risk confusing the issue with too many perspectives and humiliating your child by going public. Trust your judgment without "proof" from others.
6. Deliver a consequence that is both unemotional and stern. Tie the consequence to the action. For example, if your child used her phone to harass someone, she should lose her phone privilege. If she stood on the sidelines during a soccer game and made harassing comments, she should volunteer to clean up trash after the soccer game.
7. Do not make your kid apologize publicly or in person, unless you have approval from the target first. Parents commonly say, "I made him go to her house and apologize to her in person" as if that is the ultimate in punishment. This scenario makes me cringe for the girl who was targeted, who might

rather die than have this boy show up and fake a sincere apology. Begin with a phone call apology (and yes, I'd make him script it out to be sure it's substantive and I'd stand over his shoulder during the call) and include in the phone call, "I'd like to apologize to you in person as well, but I didn't want to upset you by showing up unannounced."

When parenting a child who knowingly hurts others, keep in mind that he is probably hurting in some way, too. Of course, the behavior is unacceptable and must be addressed. But addressing the problem with compassion will allow you to understand the behavior better in order to solve the problem, not just punish it.

#7

Camis, Tight Jeans, and Booty Shorts, Oh My!

Dodging Fashion Battles with Your Middle Schooler

My daughter came downstairs this morning before school wearing the weirdest, most unflattering outfit ever. How do I get her to change into something reasonable without starting WWIII?

In the interest of full disclosure, I should tell you that I once wore diaper pants, a bolero jacket, and a brooch to school in ninth grade. *All at the same time.* In my defense, I had a pretty big perm, so I needed volume on the lower half to add balance. And for a while I was really into wearing paint-spattered overalls with one strap hanging down. No, I was not in preschool during this phase.

I imagine if you were to flip through some of your childhood photo albums you might find a few gems of your own. Perhaps you'd even say to your own mom, "I can't believe you let me dress like that!" Isn't it funny how quickly we forget that (1) we, too, looked a little idiotic in middle school and (2) our parents weren't "letting" us make those fashion faux pas. They were cringing and complaining right before our very eyes, but we weren't seeing or hearing any of it.

We've covered how important it is for your kid to develop a unique identity during the middle school years. What could be an easier way to try on new identities than through trying on new clothes? Unfortunately, this means things start to get a little weird for a while.

The sooner you realize you cannot control your child's sense of style, and that your child's sense of style is *not a reflection on you*, the happier you'll be. I happen to live in a city where seersucker suits and pastels have always been a big part of our fashion landscape. We might be the Lilly Pulitzer capital of the world, but I've always been more a black T-shirt and old jeans kind of girl. When my kids were little, I was shocked to see kindergartner boys come to school still dressed in monogrammed, smocked, gingham rompers. Once a mom said to me, "It's just so hard to find them in his size!" and I had to suppress a spit take with my iced tea. They may have gotten away with it then, but forcing a tween into clothes they don't like is nearly impossible. If you do win that battle, it comes with a price. Either you deal with the attitude you get in return, or you watch as your kid gives in to his lack of power and personal expression. I don't like either outcome.

> Your tween is no longer your best accessory, and as soon as your kid has an opinion on what she wants to wear, I encourage you to go with the flow.

Having said all of this about staying out of style preferences, you should absolutely have rules and guidelines about modesty and respect when it comes to dressing.

Decide on your own (or with the help of friends) a few rules you'll have with regard to how your tween dresses. Then, *well before* you go shopping, talk with your son or daughter about the rules. If you wait until you're at the mall to bring up what isn't allowed, you'll have a meltdown on your hands.

Here is one way to structure your kid's fashion choices while still giving him freedom of choice. Think about types of events your child may need to attend and give him choices within these. I've broken my family's events into three DEFCON-type categories, because sometimes it feels like I'm trying to avoid a possible World War III instead of fashion crises.

Dress Code DEFCON Levels:

DEFCON Three: A Level Three event is a free-for-all, and your clothes may even get ruined. Perhaps you are playing in the creek, building houses with Habitat for Humanity, or painting a masterpiece. Wear whatever you want that you won't miss too much when it's ripped, stained, or spoiled.

DEFCON Two: Most events in life are Level Two. Going to school, a friend's house for dinner, or out to the movies are all Level Two.

- For girls: pair tight and loose. If you wear leggings, pair it with a loose top. If you wear a tank on top, pair it with a loose skirt. (This may be a guideline, not a rule.)
- No clothing with offensive or sexually suggestive words or images.
- Tanks are fine, but no camisoles without top shirts.
- No shorts or skirts that reveal too much when you bend over.
- No shirts that reveal too much when you lean forward. Use a camisole if needed.
- No odors or offensive stains.

DEFCON One: These are important or ritualized events like going to the theater, going to a party at your mom's boss's house, or having dinner at a fancy restaurant. Perhaps for your family it includes going to weekly worship or visiting a grandparent. Level Three would encompass everything included in Level Two plus:

- A collared shirt for boys.
- Nothing with writing on it.
- A dress, skirt, nice pants, or long "fancy" shorts for girls.
- Nothing that is purchased from an athletic store or in the athletic section.
- A pre-event shower.

Customize your DEFCON fashion levels as you see fit for your family. The important thing is that you have these rules established before you start trying on, or buying, clothes for middle school. Without some pre-shopping guidance, dressing room meltdowns often turn into "I hate my body!" or "You won't let me wear anything!"

If you have these levels established before you go shopping, you can tell your kid to choose most things for Level Two and a few things for Level One. You can still give her leeway to express her style within Levels Two and One as long as she's following the rules. If your kid has the levels printed out ahead of time, she can bring it to the dressing room with her. That's easier than you saying "no" over and over, and her starting to cry; let her decide for herself what passes based on your list.

If you experience frequent clothing meltdowns at your house, here are some things you can do:

1. Establish clothing guidelines and rules early, before a shopping trip.
2. See your kid's fashion choices as healthy experiments in choice and identity, not reflections on your parenting or your personal style.
3. Be lenient when it comes to clothing choice, but enforce guidelines for appropriate choices depending on the occasion or event.
4. Remember your own middle school fashion blunders and couch your clothing rules in empathy. "You know you have

a lot of freedom when it comes to what you wear, but that is a little low when you bend over. Please add a tank under that and I won't say another word except that, by the way, that skirt looks great on you."

One closing thought: no matter what your child's fashion choices, never relate clothing to body types. Your daughter doesn't want to hear that she has "your hips" and you've found that looser skirts work better for your body type. She wants to wear the skinny jeans everyone else is wearing. Let her. You may think they look terrible, and they very well may, but wearing them for a season is going to do her less harm than hearing your voice for the next thirty years whenever she thinks her hips are too wide. She'll figure out what works best for her body just like everyone else does, through trial and error after error after error.

#8

Your "Sneaking" Suspicions

Reacting to a Kid Who Goes Behind Your Back

My daughter asked to borrow my expensive new shirt and I said no. This morning, she ran out of the house with her jacket zipped to her chin and I can't find my shirt in my closet. Should I kill her? Or should I ground her first, and then kill her?

This scenario unfolds in houses across the country millions of times throughout middle school. It's not always the stolen shirt. It could be the makeup put on at school, the cell phone sneaked into class, or the movie watched without permission. You told your kid not to do something, so he did it behind your back.

Just as I'm constantly chorusing, "That's normal!" about our kids' rebellion, here I want to reassure you. The desire to react swiftly and powerfully, with long-term consequences, is entirely normal on your part.

First things first; take a breath. Because this didn't happen under your nose, you probably have a little time to formulate your response. Even though a public humiliation, such as a bust at the bus stop, would feel oh-so-good, it's not going to get the result you're after. You want guilt, and enough of it that it won't happen again. If you respond with drama, your kid will be too busy saving face to feel guilty.

Your child may act like she has power to disobey, but you still have all the actual power here. Remembering that will help you maintain the level of cool you'll need to address this. The moment you flip out, your kid will turn the focus to your reaction instead of her transgression. You have to stay cool to keep the focus on what she did wrong. I know this may be the opposite of your instinct in this situation. Trust me.

In this scenario, you believe your daughter is at school wearing your shirt, but without proof you can't accuse her. You'll lose all your credibility for future situations if you jump the gun and make an inaccurate accusation.

First, put yourself in a position to see the shirt before she can get to her room and take it off. There is nothing wrong with seeming omnipresent right now. Show up at school to drop something off. Pick her up at the bus stop to take her for ice cream. (Aren't you a sweet mom?) Offer to wash her jacket right away. Then insist. Appear helpful even if your motive is to see that shirt on her body.

For these special moments when you want to go ballistic, it may be helpful to channel a role model. Think of a character from film or TV who never loses her cool no matter who is egging her on. Maybe one of these will work for you:

Cool Hand Luke
Mary Poppins
Any Clint Eastwood character
Katniss Everdeen
Nanny McPhee
John McClane in *Die Hard*
Andy Taylor in *The Andy Griffith Show*
Clair Huxtable
James Bond
Spock
Albus Dumbledore

Minerva McGonagall
Maria in *The Sound of Music*
Atticus Finch

Choose whoever resonates with you most, and channel that character any time you discipline your middle schooler so you can stay calm and keep the upper hand.

If you don't get proof of wrongdoing, you can hint at the infraction. Again, flying off the handle without proof makes you look foolish. Hinting at the problem and possible consequence makes you look all knowing and powerful. For example, you might say, "I was thinking about the conversation we had earlier. Do you remember the one where you asked if you could borrow my shirt and I said no? Well, I was just thinking, and I'm not sure *why* I'm thinking so much about that shirt today, but I was thinking it would be very upsetting if you took something of mine without asking. Just like you wouldn't want me taking your stuff without asking, right?"

Let her squirm. Then close with "Well, there's probably no reason to spend too much time on it, but I thought it was worth mentioning one more time, that I don't want you to borrow that shirt. I can't imagine what I'd do if you were to go behind my back. Okay?"

If she took the shirt, which you know she did even though you don't have proof, you have just filled her with guilt and fear. Want to add some weight to it? You could add the pity moment. Something like, "It's just that lately I haven't been feeling good about my clothes. I'm in a slump. But that shirt is one of the few that makes me feel pretty when I put it on. I planned to wear it today because I needed an extra boost. You know how that is, right? Anyway, I guess I must have misplaced it because it wasn't in my closet."

You're telling your kid you know what happened and that you're smart and strong enough not to get caught convicting her without evidence. This should cause her great concern to be messing with a mom so smart and careful.

But let's say you do have evidence. You catch her stepping off the bus in your shirt or you get her to take that jacket off right in front of you. Now what?

Now you don't need to hint around anymore. This is where you can actually set the consequence. When I'm setting consequences, I try to get to the root of the infraction to tie the consequence to the actual problem. For example, you might be tempted to tie the consequence to clothing here, for example, "To pay me back for the shirt, you'll need to do my laundry for a week." Or you might go straight for the most popular of middle school punishments and take away her cell phone. But none of these gets to the root of the problem. At the core is now a basic mistrust. In this situation I might say, "You violated my trust and now you need to build that trust back up. Until I feel that you're trustworthy again I'll need you to stick close to home so I can keep an eye on you. When you've shown me I can trust you again, you'll get more freedom. That means no staying after school Friday to watch the football game, and you'll stay in this weekend, too. Go ahead and cancel any plans you've made."

If you find out your kid has gone behind your back and disobeyed you, here are some things you can do:

1. Take several deep breaths before taking action.
2. Don't punish based on a hunch.
3. Tie the consequence to the root of the problem.
4. Channel your favorite character to dispense unflappable discipline.
5. Spend some time thinking about what motivated your kid's decision, to see if he needs help.

Here's the thing. Your kid is going to sneak around you some. You can't expect a middle schooler to want to tell you everything. It would be worth some thought as to what's motivating her behavior. Maybe this move was impulsive only. (Remember the brain development chapter?) Maybe it was an attempt to define herself apart from you. (Remember the identity chapter?) And maybe this was really, really important to her. Use this episode as an opportunity to figure out what made this important. Is she trying to impress someone at school? Is she embarrassed her other clothes don't fit her well? Is she being teased for the brands she wears? If you can get to the root of a bigger issue, this incident may prove to be more useful than aggravating.

#9

Can You Hear Me Now?

Living in a Cell Phone World,
with a Cell Phone Boy or Girl

My ten-year-old is begging me for a cell phone. The more he tells me he's the only kid who doesn't have one, the more I want to dig in my heels and make him wait. Surely he's *not* the only one. And, more to the point, I don't want him to be spoiled. Is a cell phone really necessary at this age?

Because middle school marks so many beginnings, I am often asked, "What is the right age to let my child [fill-in-the-blank]?" From shaving to social media, boy–girl parties to cell phones, there are a lot of firsts flying at parents of tweens. For each of these decisions, you'll assess your values and determine what's practical and appropriate. I do, however, want to make a case for helping kids be socially relevant among their peers. In middle school, no kid wants to be different. Whether your child is expressing it to you or not, every day he thinks about and evaluates whether he is normal compared with the kids around him. Even the most popular and seemingly well-balanced kids in middle school worry about not being normal. Their developing bodies, brains, and identities cause them a lot of worry. Letting him have a cell phone can be an easy way to help him feel he is socially normal among his peers.

So, what is the right age to let your child own a cell phone?

Cell phones, like most of your parenting choices, should be dictated by your child's maturity level. Cell phones can be expensive. The first thing to consider is, will my child lose a phone within a week? (Every child will lose a phone at some point.) If you think your child can hang on to a phone for at least six months, that's a reasonable start. Start out with the cheapest phone you can find to test the waters.

On the subject of cheap phones, I recommend you pay for your child's first phone because then ownership is yours and you may govern its use as you see fit. If your child pays for the phone, you open yourself up to arguments about ownership and property rights. There is nothing less fun than arguing with a child who lacks logic and evidence but not energy! I do, however, suggest that your child pay for his added phone line.

The next thing to consider is, does your child *need* a cell phone? Will he use it to call you when practice has ended? Does she enter the house alone after school? Or perhaps it would be used strictly for socializing. Even if it is purely a social tool, remember that at this age of social and emotional development, being socially connected and socially appropriate are needs, not wants.

I know. You still want an age. Here it is: sixth grade.

If money and maturity are not a concern, I suggest that entering sixth grade is a reasonable time for cell phone ownership. (I'm perfectly fine with going a little younger if your family needs it to stay connected.) Transitioning into middle school is a great time to acknowledge kids' new maturity and responsibility requirements. Knowing your kid has a cell phone should give you more comfort in letting her bike to school or wander the neighborhood. I strongly believe middle schoolers don't get enough of this kind of freedom. (See problem #11: It's a Great, Big World out There (Emphasis on *Great*.)

Whether or not you're likely to give your kids that kind of independence, consider these other benefits to having a cell in middle school:

- The start and end time to sports practice or after school activities is often flexible. It's nice being in touch when plans shift.
- Kids start to make social plans by themselves. If your daughter does not have a phone, she may be left out of the planning. No, she's not the master planner that you are, but now is a good time to learn.
- Phones are a great tool to teach self-reliance and problem solving ("Your ride didn't show up and I'm at work. Who are you going to call?"), money management (lots of kids pay for the added phone line), and confidence/etiquette ("Can you please call Aunt Mary and ask what we can bring to the party?").

Common concerns I hear about letting kids have cell phones are:

- "It opens up a terrifying new world of cyber bullying."
- "It's not a necessity."
- "I don't want to raise overindulged kids."
- "I don't want to raise kids who never look up from screens."

These are fair and reasonable concerns. Not allowing cell phones, however, may not be a fair and reasonable solution. When it comes to technology, I suggest parents worry less about what the technology can do and think more about what they, as parents, can do to make the technology work for them.

As the parent, put restrictions on cell phone use to address your concerns. Here are some that I like:

1. If there is a password on the phone, I must always know it. If you change the password and don't tell me, there will be a consequence.
2. I may look at your texts at any time. Only text things you are okay with me seeing. I will respect your privacy and only discuss a text with you if I have safety or moral concerns.

3. Your cell phone cannot be in your room after eight o'clock at night. It must be recharging in the kitchen at that time.

4. This is new to us both and we're both learning. I can change the family rules around cell phone use as needed to address new situations as they arise.

Creating and modifying rules around etiquette and safety are a more effective way of raising kids who are responsible, thoughtful communicators in this technical age than a blanket "no" to technology.

If you're on the verge of breaking the cell phone barrier, here are some things to consider:

1. Think carefully about what frightens you most when it comes to technology and honestly assesses the reality of your concerns.

2. Use parenting skills (limitations, rules, and communication) to mitigate concerns associated with technology, rather than banning technology altogether.

3. Don't worry about what other parents might think about your choices.

4. Don't bash other parents' choices either.

5. Establish rules and expectations for technology use before introducing the device to the child.

6. Casually monitor use.

7. Have a good time with your kid. Send texts occasionally instead of having a conversation. Snap funny pictures and share them. Prank call your kid! Have a little fun.

8. Understand that learning how to properly use technology is essential to this generation and that making mistakes when learning how to do something new is essential to human nature.

#10

Going Out, Going Nowhere

Understanding the Middle School Dating Scene

I read some texts on my daughter's phone between her and a boy that obviously mean they're "going out." I think sixth grade is way too young to be boyfriend and girlfriend! Am I crazy?

"Boyfriend and girlfriend" are loosely defined terms that scare parents because they can mean so many different things. If I stood two cute sixth graders in front of a room full of parents and told them these kids are "going out," the parent reactions would range from adoring smiles to cringes to screams of "Noooo!"

The "looseness" of this term means you can imagine it to mean anything, your worst nightmare or your sweetest hope. Rather than defining your child's social life around a moving target, get specific about what "going out" really means and what aspects, if any, you'll allow this year.

I'll help you get specific in a minute, but first, consider this: you have very little power over whom your son or daughter finds attractive, and when that will happen. This is true for friends as much as it is for fledgling romantic relationships.

> Friendships are a precursor to romantic relationships. Once your kid goes to middle school, you can't pick his friends for him, but you can lay the foundation for self-respect.

Because girlfriend/boyfriend issues are so closely tied to friendship issues, let's look at what's happening with friend selection in middle school as the foundation for how you might react to romantic relationships.

In middle school, your kid will begin spending more time with people you don't like. Maybe you'll know about this and maybe you won't. (If you're on social media watching your kid's accounts, you'll definitely be more likely to find out.) But what do you do with that information? You may believe another kid to be a bad influence, but resist the urge to ban your child from hanging out with certain kids.

> When it comes to your kid's choices in friends, I suggest you limit activities, not people.

There is no better way to make a kid more appealing than to make him off-limits. If you are not comfortable with another child's choices or values, but your child wants to be friends with that kid, invite him to your house where you can keep an eye on his influence. It's not a good idea to say, "You can't be friends with Will." It's more effective to say, "You can't go roller skating with Will Friday night. You can invite him to go to the movies with us instead." Offer to sit in another row. If your child questions you on this, be honest. Say something like, "I don't know Will very well and I'm concerned about some of his behaviors and choices. I need to get to know him better."

You can avoid the draw of forbidden fruit by allowing your child's friend into his life on your terms. Not only does banning people backfire, but you *could* be wrong about the person. Or the friend could change. And your kid will be spending time with him at school, without you, anyway. To modify an old saying, "Keep your child's sweet friends close. Keep your child's suspect friends closer."

Boyfriends and girlfriends are really just an extension of friends. At this age you can say, "You're not allowed to date," but unless you've been specific with your child about what that means, you could be setting yourself up for failure.

Let's get specific by defining what "going out" means. You may be the parent who screams "Noooo!" because you're imagining something different than what your child has in mind.

Would it seem appropriate to you if your daughter:

- Sat next to a boy at lunch?
- Held hands with a boy?
- Called someone her boyfriend but never went out alone with him outside of school?
- Went to the movie with a boy and a parent chaperone?
- Had her first kiss?

You get the idea. Spend some time narrowing down what you do and don't want her to do, and talk with her about it. Better yet, ask your son or daughter what it means to her to "go out with someone." When your kid defines "going out" for you, it may alleviate your worry *and* the need to set a lot of rules. While you're at it, ask if "going out" is even the right term anymore. If you keep using the wrong term your kid will cringe every time you try to talk about it. What used to be "going steady" evolved to "going out" but now a lot of middle schoolers call it "talking to" someone, which really means texting with someone. You get the idea.

I'm not suggesting you can mandate your kid's behavior when she's not with you. But I am certain you can help guide her thinking. One of the reasons parents don't do this is because it treads into some really uncomfortable territory, namely...budding sexuality. You don't actually get to circle a date on the calendar when your daughter will start kissing but you can help her consider when, where, and maybe even how it would be appropriate to start down that road. Since that's about all you can do, I recommend not missing out on your only opportunity to influence this big decision. Bear in mind that most kids kiss for the first time in middle school. That doesn't mean your kid *will* kiss in middle school (or for that matter that you need to approve) but you should be honest with yourself about this societal norm.

Lest you should think I'm too flimsy on this subject, let me be clear that you still (mostly) get to decide where your kid goes outside of school time, for how long, under what circumstances, and with whom. What you don't get to decide is whether or not they make out by the water fountain after third period.

If your son or daughter wants to "go out" or "talk to" someone and that means a little texting back and forth or nervously standing together at the middle school football game, it's not a big deal. But, if your kid jumps from relationship to relationship or spends a lot of time with a boyfriend or girlfriend at the exclusion of other people, activities, or schoolwork, I would put on the brakes. In a 2013 study[1] from the University of Georgia, researchers found that kids who began dating in early middle school and continued with high frequency had worse study skills than their peers and were twice as likely to drink or do drugs later in adolescence. The correlation, researchers believe, is a tendency to be drawn to higher-risk behaviors. Therefore, I would delay unnecessary risk taking for that child as long as possible, especially given that romantic relationships also affect reputations, academics, and friendships.

If your child is not dating habitually, here are some good things to come out of the *occasional* middle school relationship:

- Having a boyfriend or girlfriend may give your tween some personal and social confidence.

- It gives your child practice in relating to the opposite sex.
- It allows kids to show a different side of their personality to the opposite sex; for example, boys don't have to play the tough guy and girls get to escape from girl drama.

If your kid wants to have a boyfriend or girlfriend, here are some things you can do:

1. Ask your kid what it means to "go out" with someone.
2. Accept that this is a natural developmental progression.
3. Define the parameters of the situation.
4. Put reasonable limits on when and where your child goes with friends.
5. Accept that your child will make lots of relationship decisions on his own.
6. If your child is willing, talk with her early—before relationships are even on her radar—about what qualities she would look for in a boyfriend and which would be deal breakers.
7. Model respectful relationships by pointing out the respectful things your partner does for you, that you see friends doing for each other, or that you see while watching TV or movies. While you're at it, point out examples of disrespect in relationships, too, so your child will have a gage for what a respectful relationship looks like before he starts dating.

#11

It's a Great, Big World out There (Emphasis on Great)

Evaluating How Much Independence to Give Your Middle Schooler

My son wants to ride his bike two miles to the shopping center alone. I'd feel better if he rode with a group of friends but my husband thinks that's ridiculous. How much independence is too much at this age?

Just as you might expect, I need to start my response with the standard, "This answer will vary for every family based on your child's maturity level, your neighborhood, and your unique circumstances." You know your child and personal situation better than I. So, let's consider that box checked and move on to what you really need to hear.

The adage that there is safety in numbers is generally true for lots of stages in our lives, but not necessarily in adolescence. Remember chapter 2, when I wrote about that study done by Laurence Steinberg at Temple University? The study showed that when faced with the same risk-provoking scenarios as adults, teens who were *alone* took no more risks than adults. But, teens who were with a friend took far more risks than they did when they were alone. The desire to be perceived as cool, competent, edgy, and brave by their peers is more important to teens than the fear of being hurt, grounded, or screamed at by a parent or police officer. The adolescent brain is programmed to seek out social acceptance by peers, not to follow social rules constructed by adults.

Before you hang your head in defeat, let me also remind you why this is. Your child must begin to find a future for herself in a world that will soon be run by her peers. If she doesn't figure out early on ways to be impressive on her own, she sets herself up to live with you forever and ever. Hide your ice cream and TV remote. That kid's going nowhere.

While it may be painful to recognize that taking risks is, by design, an important part of being an adolescent, it helps to remember that your end goal is to raise kids who know how and when to take the kind of good risks (going to college, getting a job) that get them off your couch.

At the root of your question about independence is probably a very normal fear of being responsible for something bad happening to your child. We live in an age when we are inundated with news stories of horrific crimes happening against children. I bet most parents have an unhealthy fear of their child being abducted. But how likely is it to happen? In America, the chance of your kid being abducted by a stranger is .00007 percent.

It seems much, much higher, doesn't it? That's because we hear about abductions and other child crimes all the time on the news, at a rate disproportionate to their likelihood of happening. Someone in, or close to, the family commits most child kidnappings. You let your kid hang out with family and friends, right? Without a doubt, it would be the worst thing in the world for your child to be taken by a stranger, but I guarantee that you expose your kids to more dangerous possibilities every single day of their lives. I know parents who keep their kids virtually under house arrest for fear of strangers, and I think that's sad. To put your mind at ease, I recommend you read Lenore Skenazy's book, *Free-Range Kids*.

Maybe you're afraid of a more likely bad ending to a bike ride to the store: the possibility of your son riding into traffic and getting hit by a car. This is a reasonable thing to worry about and there are two things you can do to improve his safety record: (1) Before you allow him to bike places, make sure he has experience riding with you or another adult and shows good understanding of traffic rules. It's one thing for him to tell you he knows the rules but it's another for you to see him in action, especially when you see him do the right thing in a confusing situation. (2) Don't send him with a friend he wants to impress.

Besides it just being fun, there are lots of reasons older kids need time away from their parents. A tween's middle school years are all about developing an identity apart from his parents. This is hard to do when you have a set of watchful eyes on you all the time. It is hard to become your own person when you feel that your every decision is being evaluated and judged. Have you ever been micromanaged? It makes it difficult to be successful. Kids need time apart from their parents to figure out who they are independently of their parents, and to develop a strong sense of self.

The second reason is that independence builds competency. Kids naturally do better at things when they don't feel parental pressure. Not surprisingly, they become better problem solvers when they actually get to practice solving problems. In his book *Homesick and Happy*, Michael Thompson, PhD, tells us that in asking thousands of adults to recall the "sweetest memory" from their childhood, 80 percent recalled a time when their parents were not present.[1] Kids need and want to overcome challenges on their own so they can feel successful and capable of taking care of themselves. This is what we want, too, right? Just checking.

If you are struggling with letting your child become more independent, here are some things you can do:

1. Learn the facts about child safety and realize that the world is generally a safe place for your child.

2. Let your kid enjoy that world by giving her permission to go outside into it, sometimes alone.

3. Teach your kid basic safety rules like how to negotiate traffic, how to respond if harassed, and how (and who) to ask for help.

4. Begin teaching your kids to have a confident voice at an early age. "Confident" means strong, loud, and clear. This starts simply with things like ordering for themselves at restaurants or asking adults in stores where to find the restroom. Resist the urge to do it for them! This helps them to be confident and mature communicators. In the very *(very)* rare cases of strangers who abduct kids, they look for the easiest targets and those are kids who won't talk back, or say no, or use a loud, confident voice.

I know that "independence" can be a scary concept but I encourage you to seek, create, embrace, and celebrate opportunities for your child to do brave things alone. These events create memories your kid can be proud of because they strengthen your child's level of responsibility and confidence.

#12

"Get Him out of My Room!"

Dealing with Sibling Fights and Manipulations

My thirteen-year-old daughter has been nasty to her younger brother recently. She snaps at him, makes fun of him, provokes him, and then claims we're being unfair when we intervene. I can't stand living in a house with so much tension. I never know if the "sweet girl" or the "rude teen" is going to show up each day. How can I get her to see that she's behaving miserably?

The short answer is, don't intervene. I know it seems like a total injustice against your son not to interfere, but what I mean is, don't intervene *obviously* and definitely not right away.

Your daughter may be acting up for lots of reasons. Usually, when someone has a radical shift in behavior like you're describing, she's holding in tension from somewhere else and letting it out in the safest place possible. Lucky you. Your daughter may be lashing out because she's hurt. Punishing her may stop her behavior in the short term, but it won't fix the root of her problems. Or maybe she just likes pushing her brother's buttons. In that case, he needs to learn how to react in a way that doesn't give her what she wants.

So, let's use this opportunity to coach your son on how to blow off someone who is being a jerk. These skills will empower him to handle these situations in school and, hopefully, he won't need you (as much) to intervene with his sister. Take him aside, perhaps for ice cream or on a special walk together, and let him know you've noticed how his sister is behaving. Explain to your son that his sister's behavior is her problem, not his. He'll probably ask (demand) that you do something. "Punish her, already!" Maybe he won't care, but maybe he'll feel better knowing this is her problem, not his.

Next, coach him on ways he can respond that will show his sister he is unflustered by her absurd behavior, sort of the little brother version of "Botox Brow."

He could:

- Smile and leave
- Agree with her (how disarming!)
- Ask her politely if she's okay
- Apologize
- Shrug

Any of these may initially cause your daughter to scream with frustration because she isn't getting the reaction she wanted. But after a few times, she'll learn that her brother is not the easy target she once thought. If your son can stick with a neutral response, he'll get paid off tremendously when his sister backs off for good. These are the same skills that can work with bullies, mean friends, and other adversaries.

On the other hand, let's suppose her behavior is indicative of something bigger. If she's lashing out because in another area of her life (friends, school, maybe even parents) she feels powerless and angry, she needs more than stonewalling. She could use a little empathy, too.

Once the heat of the moment dissipates, approach your daughter to talk about her behavior. Rather than being accusatory, try a softer start, something like, "I'm sorry you got upset with your brother. You seemed so upset. It made me wonder if there's something else bothering you? I'm here to listen if you ever want to talk about friends, school, family, or anything else on your mind. Sometimes it helps just to get it off your chest. I love you."

She may or may not be ready to talk right then and there. But she'll remember that you're ready to listen. She'll also know you're keeping an eye on her behavior.

If all else fails and her nasty behavior is unbearable, you can move on to step three. Antisocial behavior gets antisocial consequences. You can approach her quietly and privately to say something like this:

> I've noticed you're still being disrespectful to your brother, and I've watched him try to take it without turning it into a fight. I've asked you if something bigger is bothering you and I'm still here anytime to listen when you want to talk. But it's becoming unbearable to listen to you being so rude. I'd love for you to join us when you can talk respectfully to everyone in this family. Until then, you can spend time in your room alone with a good book.

Take away technology and any special events she was planning on. When she's ready to talk respectfully, you will be happy to give those back. The key is to sound calm and pleasant as you say all of this so she can get to calm and pleasant herself.

A note on sibling rivalry: It's not your job to ensure that your kids like each other. It's not even your job to make sure they get along. That's *their* job. The more neutral you are, without making any comparisons between them, the more likely they won't make comparisons between themselves. That will naturally lead to a more peaceful, hopefully even fun, sibling relationship.

If your kids fight often and fight hard, here are some things you can do:

1. Separate them. Literally put them in neutral corners and separate rooms.
2. Wait before reacting to sibling arguments.
3. Approach kids separately and privately about behavior related to siblings.
4. Try very hard not to make comparisons between siblings.
5. Coach your kids to respond to provocative siblings without escalating drama.
6. Express empathy for the child who is angry as well as the child who is being targeted.
7. React to antisocial behavior with antisocial consequences.

#13
Going at Different Speeds

Helping Your Socially Immature Kid Find a
Comfortable Place in Middle School

**My daughter's friends are interested in boys and vampire
novels. My daughter still plays with Barbies. Is she going to
get eaten alive in middle school? Help.**

I can remember the exact moment in sixth grade when my friend
Hannah stopped wanting to play the same way I did. We used to
run home after school to catch the second half of *Days of Our Lives*.
During the commercial breaks we would play a game we called
"Teachers," an imaginative game in which we would act out skits
that mocked our teachers. They might unexpectedly fart during a lesson, or have crushes on each other, or consume food loudly, or other
human things that cracked us up because teachers weren't real people.

When we played Teachers I would belly laugh until it hurt. One
commercial break I hopped up to act out a skit and Hannah said,
"Let's not play Teachers. It's getting boring." I remember not knowing what to do with myself. "It's not boring," I replied. Everything
felt surreal. Was I in some kind of alternate universe where the game
Teachers was *not* awesome? I couldn't wrap my brain around it. I
tried reminding Hannah how funny it was by jumping into a fresh
skit but she didn't laugh. "We can just watch the commercials until
the show comes back on," she said, staring past me at the TV.

I sat there, slumped into the old basement couch, watching ads for tampons and fabric softener and other womanly things and thought, "No, *this* is boring. She's wrong. Playing Teachers is fun." But I knew from Hannah's tone and expression that no amount of persuasion would convince her that we should play as we had only days ago, doubled over and clutching our bellies as we laughed at our ridiculous skits, when what she really wanted to do was learn how to get rid of blackheads and be more attractive to boys.

I was mad at Hannah at the time, and then hurt, but the truth is that in middle school kids develop at vastly different speeds and there is nothing wrong with that. There is also very little you, as a parent, can do about it. Take a stroll down a middle school hallway and it's easy to spot the physical developmental differences. Some kids look like third graders and some look like they should be driving.

> After her first day of sixth grade I asked my daughter, "So, was there anything that surprised you about middle school?" and she replied flatly, "Yeah. Mustaches."

Even as adults we take for granted the vast physical difference among middle schoolers. Imagine all the social and emotional differences lurking beneath the surface. Because those are harder to see, it's easy to assume that the girls reading vampire novels and reapplying eyeliner after gym are the norm. Chances are, though, that in the vast sea of middle school kids there are girls just like yours who still think of makeup as "dress up" and would rather brush their doll's hair than their own.

Boys struggle with this, too, though usually not as much because boys actually *are* less socially mature than girls in middle school. There is about a two- to three-year gap in brain development between the genders during the middle school years, so younger play is still more socially acceptable among boys. For many boys, throwing a ball is the universal and timeless social equalizer so having a catch at recess, or with a wadded up piece of paper before class, is something most boys, regardless of maturity level, can do together. Some boys do get girl crazy earlier than the rest of the pack, though, and these boys often lead the social scene early in middle school. Not only are they interested in girls, they actually text and talk with them, make plans, and eventually are among the first to ask someone out. Once a few boys take the lead here, they often start teasing boys who are less interested in girls, probably as a way to normalize their own desires.

Not all boys enjoy throwing a ball, just as not all girls like boys and vampire novels. Because it's not cool to broadcast less socially mature interests, these kids can have a harder time finding and connecting with each other. I knew a mom whose daughter was intellectually superior to most in her class, but socially far behind. She had highly developed interests and hobbies, but no friends to discuss them with. Not surprisingly, she spent a lot of her "social time" with teachers, who appreciated her intelligence and didn't mind (perhaps even enjoyed) that she wasn't a rabid One Direction fan.

One of her daughter's favorite book series was *Lord of the Rings*. It's not an easy thing to launch into at the cafeteria table when everyone else is talking about YouTube videos. In a brilliant yet subtle marketing move, her mom had a necklace made for her with an Elvin symbol on it. Not only was it a great conversation starter whenever someone asked about her unusual and pretty necklace, but it was a beacon for other kids who liked the books, too, and it ultimately helped her make a connection with another die-hard fan at her school.

Aside from something like this, the best thing you can do is to be patient. Social maturity can't be cajoled out of kids so enjoy this extra time spent with your daughter and her dolls. Eventually she'll put them away for more adult pursuits and you may find yourself wishing you hadn't fretted away these delicate years. Plus, if you're worrying about this, your daughter is going to pick up on it. Even when parents make an effort not to telegraph their concerns, the kids always pick up on subtle clues, like seemingly innocent questions that all focus on themes like friends, popularity, fitting in, or generally "being happy." Your child may be cataloguing the number of times you say things like "Who did you sit with at lunch?" and "Kate seems like a nice girl. Why don't you invite her over?" and "What do the other kids talk about?" The less you seem invested in her social happiness, the happier she'll be.

> You might think that you are encouraging your child to be more social by asking subtle questions about his peer interactions, but to him it probably feels more like pressure to perform than a gentle inquiry.

Parents who try to compensate for their kids' social differences often further delay their progress. Shy kids, for example, are not socially immature. They're shy. Parents who speak for them only make their kids feel worse and less inclined to speak for themselves. Parents who try to be the "life of the middle school party," cracking jokes with their kids' classmates at sporting events or in car-pool line, aren't bridging any gaps between their child and his peers. They're only making their reserved kid uncomfortable. Stay neutral and your kid will find a spot just right for her.

> Some parents are naturally cool and kids get that, but it is rare that parental coolness is transferred by osmosis to kids, unless you are a recognizable celebrity. Otherwise, middle schoolers see parents as a different species with nontransferable qualities. Trying to win cool points *for* your kid doesn't work.

If you're concerned for your child's social development and acceptance at school, here are some things you can do:

1. Enjoy your child for who she is today not who you hope she'll become, and try to cross this off your list of things to worry about. Your child will sense your anxiety and internalize it.

2. Remember that during middle school kids develop on a wider time range than at any other time of life. Be patient.

3. Help your kid broadcast subtle signals to his peers about his unique interests. CafePress.com is a great website for ordering custom tees, bags, jewelry, and countless other types of swag.

4. Don't confuse shyness with immaturity and certainly don't try to "fix" it by forcing your kid to be more talkative or by talking for him. Set minimal expectations for mandatory politeness like making eye contact, shaking hands with adults, and saying thank you loudly enough that everyone can hear. Beyond that, don't do much else.

5. If your kid is socially immature but excels in other areas, encourage her to get involved in a school organization that allows her to compete for her school. Kids value success, whether it's on the soccer field or the Odyssey of the Mind team. Bringing home a win for the school will positively influence how her peers perceive her and will give her opportunities to connect with others who share similar interests, on her terms.

6. Help your kid pursue his interests. He may feel "less than" the cool kids because he doesn't like, or even *want* to like, the same things. Giving him time and space to explore the activities that bring him joy will help him feel proud. If possible, get him involved in groups that share his interests whether that's a bowling league, an art class, Boy Scouts, or skateboard lessons. He'll feel good being surrounded by people who think like him.

Finishing Touches

Your Middle-Age Construction Project

As we near the end of your Middle School Makeover it's time for the finishing touches. Last, but definitely not least, let's talk about you.

While your middle schooler is busy working on the three major construction projects of adolescence—building a new body, brain, and identity—you're doing the same thing, whether you realize it or not.

> Parenting middle schoolers is unique in that parent and child are on similar developmental tracks. You're both undergoing major changes in body, brain, and identity at this time of life.

An important piece of being a good parent is being good to yourself first. It helps your child develop good self-care habits to see you modeling this kind of behavior and it recharges your batteries so you can have happier relationships with your family. As every good flight attendant will tell you, you must put on your own oxygen mask before putting one on your child. Let's look at some ways you can appreciate and take care of yourself first throughout this complicated phase of your life.

THE TIMES THEY ARE A-CHANGIN'

In the first chapter of this book, I referred to my survey of one hundred parents of third, fourth, and fifth graders about their expectations around parenting middle schoolers.

> A quarter of the parents I surveyed had a distinctly bad middle school experience and half of those could think of *nothing* to look forward to about their kids going to middle school.

The parents who could identify something positive to anticipate most commonly answered with a version of "new opportunities" (both social and academic) and "more independence."

It's true that heading to middle school brings your child all kinds of exciting new opportunities and independence, but...enough about them. What about you? This isn't just an important time in your adolescent's development. You're going through a lot of changes now, too, and having older kids means you get to enjoy more independence and new experiences as well.

In some ways that can be exciting, but in many ways the changes you're facing now are more daunting than delightful. You may be starting to care for your aging parents, worried about your own body's changes, considering a career change, struggling with divorce and single parenting, or facing a myriad of other issues confronting people our age. It would be difficult enough to tackle these lifestyle adjustments at any stage, but while you're trying to parent a middle schooler—yikes. That's a lot of emotional imbalance and uncertainty, all at once.

This year, I have both a sixth and eighth grader in middle school. It is also the year I had:

- Shoulder surgery
- Five root canals
- Neuroma: a nerve condition in my foot causing pain and killing my ability to wear heels (waaah!)
- Recently divorced parents
- A mother who lives alone and has had several surgeries during the year
- A husband who started traveling extensively for work
- A close friend who entered rehab and needed my support
- A growing business with all the usual demands on an entrepreneur and working mom
- A book published!

I have had a front-row seat in the theater of stress, chaos, grief, expectation, loneliness, anxiety, excitement, reinvention, doubt, helplessness, and hope that this stage of life can bring. As a parent, especially a parent to kids in a uniquely egocentric phase of life, it can feel unnatural to put yourself first. It's been said a million times before and in a million better ways, I'm sure, that being a good parent is only possible when you take care of yourself, too. If you aren't aware of some significant way in which you put yourself first, I guarantee this will come back to bite you, your relationships, and your kid.

YOUR CHANGING BODY

A few years ago, a friend and I started working out together three times a week with a trainer. Neither of us had exercised this routinely or with such effort since high school. We would encourage each other, talking about how proud we were, how good it felt to have increased strength and stamina. On a shopping trip to Target one day, my friend noticed guys were actually checking her out.

What a cool side benefit! She walked through the store with a little extra confidence and swagger. Then, in the checkout line, she saw a guy do a double take her way and she followed his eyes...right to her eighth-grade daughter's butt.

Her daughter, though just thirteen, is very tall (taller than her mom) and was faced away from the guy, so I'm not calling him a pedophile. I'm just saying, it is a weird day for a mom when she realizes that her daughter now looks old enough to draw men's attention. Take that in as you ponder this: even though we sometimes feel like it's only been a minute since high school, the world sees us as our current age, and for women, that means the world sees us less and less. As our daughters become increasingly attractive, we start to become increasingly invisible.

This phenomenon certainly isn't restricted to women. Men, too, feel the dreaded march of time as their bodies begin the process of sarcopenia, a typical 3-5% loss of muscle mass per decade for inactive adults. As middle-aged men naturally become older and softer their sons are simultaneously ascending toward the peak of their physical strength. For some men this poses a conflicting source of pride in their sons' masculinity and depression at their own loss of strength and stamina. Decline in testosterone can also increase feelings of depression around middle age.

Fathers can also feel conflicted watching their daughters become young women. Many fathers retreat as their daughters' bodies begin developing. Not wanting to be perceived as inappropriate, they stop making physical contact. Girls in middle school still crave affection from their fathers, though. Hugs, cuddles on the couch, and good night kisses remind a girl that she's still special to her dad even though she's growing up.

Dads should also know that they start having an equal or more profound impact than moms on their daughters' body image once girls hit their late teens. Older girls begin to look to their dads for cues on how women should be treated, what men value in women, what men find attractive, and what will help them be successful in the world. Body bashing and an emphasis on physical attractiveness is especially damaging coming from dads. The flip side is that dads have a tremendous opportunity to affect a positive self-image in their daughters by remarking on successful women for their non-physical attributes, refraining from making any comments—positive or negative—about women's bodies, and showing their daughters how to be treated respectfully by the opposite sex.

PLASTIC SURGERY

For some women, plastic surgery offers a way to beat the clock. I live in Charlotte, North Carolina, where you can't pick up a magazine, turn on the radio, or drive down our city streets without being hit by a barrage of ads, one after the other, for plastic surgery. Charlotte is the second-largest banking capital of the United States, after New York City. Expendable income + growing cultural pressure = lots of women paying to look like they are immune to the passage of time. It's called getting the "mommy makeover." It begins to mess with your idea of what's normal when fewer and fewer women around you have wrinkles, or belly fat, or real breasts.

I've tiptoed close to the cosmetic surgery cliff before. Once, I made it as far as the surgeon's free consultation, in which he told me I could try losing weight to get rid of my belly fat but "then my face would look like hell" so instead he recommended *four or five* procedures that could help out all around. I shared my conflicted feelings with my best friend on a visit to Boston, over wine in a hotel lobby, where she looked at me sympathetically and said, "Don't do it. That's just not who you are. You're smart and funny and pretty, and your body is just doing what bodies do."

Well. That was liberating. I had heard that sentiment many times before from self-acceptance gurus, but hearing it from my friend in such a matter-of-fact way was joyful. I think it was her telling me, "That's not who you are," that liberated me from my anxiety because the plastic surgery thing really *isn't* me but my culture was making me doubt it.

Clearly, we don't shed all our insecurities when we leave middle school behind.

Men, too, are getting in on plastic surgery trends in rapidly increasing numbers. According to the American Society of Aesthetic Plastic Surgery, a study revealed that male patients had 750,000 cosmetic procedures in 2010. That may represent a mere 8 percent of total procedures that year, but the more staggering statistic is how quickly the popularity of plastic surgery among men is rising. Since 1997, the number of cosmetic procedures performed on men has increased by 88 percent.

If you find yourself struggling with getting older, what it does to your body, your brain, or your spirit, I understand. I'm definitely not here to judge anyone who has made, or will make, the personal decision to have plastic surgery. It's not for me, but that doesn't mean it's not for you. What I hope we can all agree on, though, is that our girls, even as young as elementary school, are already beginning the work we have started at comparing our bodies and doubting our relative beauty. Because girls feel cultural pressure younger and younger to be perfect, we should look closely at what it means to be in middle school and have your parent get plastic surgery.

The most common cosmetic surgery procedure for people ages thirty-five to fifty is lipoplasty (liposuction). The most common nonsurgical procedure is Botox.[1] I have friends who've done both. I have done neither. It's neither here nor there, in our friendships. But kids in the midst of puberty and identity development are not so immune. One of the reasons I've always been personally conflicted about plastic surgery is that I have a daughter and I didn't know how to teach her to love her body any better, especially on the days she told me she wished she didn't have a fat belly, than to stop worrying about mine. After all, there are more important, certainly much more fun, places where I can devote my energy, time, and money.

If you decide that plastic surgery is the right choice for you, consider how it might impact your child's perceptions of his or her own body. Amy Combs, PsyD, founder of the Charlotte Center for Balanced Living in Charlotte, North Carolina, specializes in body acceptance and treating eating disorders, as well as other issues affecting women and girls. Dr. Combs offers the following advice for talking to your tweens about the changes they'll see in your body:

> The decision to have plastic surgery is both personal and contextual. Adults may not be entirely clear on their reasons for having the procedures, but they must convey clarity to protect their children both in terms of their personal body images as well as how they view others. Not acknowledging your personal feelings and circumstances around the decision to have surgery may set up your teen to be waiting for the day she can alter x or y about her body, without first working on developing self-acceptance.

"Ideally," says Dr. Combs, "if you decide to have plastic surgery, you will convey the following messages to your children, both male and female, about elective surgical changes."

- This is a want not a need. You want to have this procedure. You do not need to have it to have a better, happier, more meaningful life.
- You are having this procedure because of _____ (cancer, breast feeding, aging, overeating, or physical insecurity). You need to own this. One of the most difficult procedures to explain to an adolescent might be lipoplasty. You will need to acknowledge that you are having this because you are

dissatisfied with the way your body is aging/changing/not responding to diet and exercise.

- Within these discussions you should acknowledge a feeling of discomfort or insecurity with your body.

- Communicate that you are not hoping or imagining that by having this procedure other areas of your life will improve. You aren't imagining that people will like you more, your friendships or marriage will be more solid, you'll have more confidence in the workplace, etc. This is a purely *aesthetic* procedure. If you do believe these things will happen, be very careful how you communicate to your children. Eating disorders often start with highly restrictive attempts at dieting, which is a teenager's version of lipoplasty.

- A conversation about values is also essential. It might go something like this: "This decision to have elective surgery reflects my values. These do not need to be your values. You can make that decision when you are an adult. Many other women that we know have not had this type of procedure, which is reflective of their values." With this you want to make sure you choose an admired adult as a model of the decision to forgo elective surgery.

Hoping your child won't notice isn't a good plan. Once children are in middle school they become very aware of bodies and they internalize what they see in others into personal messages about themselves. The goal of being so direct is to protect your child from potentially viewing himself or herself or others as *flawed* and eventually defaulting to plastic surgery as *the solution*. Just realize that by not talking about it or assuming your teenager won't notice, you open the door to him or her relying on a teenage interpretation of a decision you yourself may have struggled with as an adult. Kids this age may not be equipped with the wisdom or life experience to successfully navigate this without your guidance.

Whatever your choice, I hope you have a level of gratitude for your body and all the things it does for you on a daily basis.

BODIES BEYOND AESTHETICS

Of course, not all the body changes we face these days are aesthetic. Many of you are embarking toward, or battling through, menopause or andropause. Some of you are fighting serious illnesses of the body or brain. These circumstances only complicate this phase of life, and the best we can do is to stay optimistic, diligent, and to be kind to ourselves, and each other, through this tangled mess of being human together.

YOUR CHANGING BRAIN

Okay, what was I gonna say here? Something about the thing?

Most of us can empathize with each other these days in the slower recollection of vocabulary and names, even our kids' names, among our set. I call my son the dog's name all the time. This slow draining of vocabulary reminds me of an episode of *The Simpsons* in which Homer and Marge have a typical middle-aged exchange:

> HOMER: Marge, where's that...metal deely...you use to... dig...food...
> MARGE: You mean, a spoon?
> HOMER: Yeah, yeah!

Sound familiar?

I laughed recently when a friend told me she was trying to get her husband on board with her idea for a home improvement project in the downstairs bathroom but she had so much going on inside her brain she couldn't recall the word for bathroom. She kept calling it the "tiny kitchen" and hoping he would understand. Needless to say, they became quickly frustrated with each other.

We all know time takes its toll on the middle-aged brain, but this wouldn't be much of a makeover if I didn't also point out a couple of great things that are happening to your brain these days. In fact, my brain is doing one of them right now.

BEING POSITIVE

In chapter 2, when I wrote about the developing middle schooler's brain, I explained that the amygdala, the emotional center of the brain, takes over brain management while the prefrontal cortex goes on its extended lunch break. In adolescence, the primary emotion of the amygdala is anger, which explains why teens are quick to snap. In older adults, the amygdala becomes less responsive to negative input and more responsive to positive input.[2] Collectively, we are at a glass-half-full stage of development. This is good news, given all the potential you have for reinvention at this stage of your life.

BETTER COGNITION

Our generation may laugh off our declining abilities—it's laugh or cry, right? Glass half full! But research shows that our cognitive abilities actually improve through middle age. Our ability to memorize and quickly process information will decline leading up to and through middle age, but our ability to reason and solve problems improves.[3] You're not becoming dumber than you were in college. You're becoming different. Better. In middle age, your brain engages both hemispheres for analyzing and solving problems, a much more well-rounded approach. So give yourself credit for your excellent, ongoing brain development.

YOUR CHANGING IDENTITY

For some of you reading this book, your child's transition to middle school is difficult because it signifies that he's heading toward greater independence, and that leaves you wondering, well, wondering where that leaves you. Assuming your child will go to college (or on some other similarly respectable pursuit) at age eighteen, you can look at your child at age ten and think, "You have now lived with me for more than half of the total time you will." At the same time, you can look yourself in the mirror and think, "With luck, I'm at the midpoint of my life today." After you scoop up your jaw, you may find yourself pondering some of life's larger questions.

- What do I do with myself now?
- Am I living the life I wanted?
- How do I make an impact?
- Have I sacrificed too much? Not enough?
- Where do I go from here?

It isn't just your middle schooler who's working on a new identity these days. Many parents reinvent themselves at this stage of life and it can be an exciting, if trepidatious, task. For many of you, the past ten-plus years have been spent giving, planning, and preparing for your child to be an independent adult someday. Yet, when your kid begins to get his social and emotional needs met elsewhere, it can leave you feeling stranded. Many parents find themselves out of the habit of taking care of themselves. It feels selfish to prioritize your own interests, especially when your child is developing so many new ones, but it is essential to your happiness, and your kid's, that you do.

In chapter 3, I wrote about Identity vs. Role Confusion, Erik Erikson's stage of psychosocial development that most middle schoolers find themselves in, during which they must begin to form an identity outside of their parents. Most parents of middle schoolers find ourselves in Erikson's seventh stage of development, which he called Generativity vs. Stagnation. During this middle adulthood stage of life, spanning from ages forty to sixty-five, we prepare to leave behind a legacy when we die so that we don't feel as though our existence has been futile.

In a biological sense, our kids, and their kids, and theirs, are our legacy. But even though our little legacies are preparing to leave us, we're not done. We've still got plenty of energy, ambition, and desire to do more. Some of you are launching new careers, rediscovering old passions, or perhaps even reinventing yourselves entirely at this stage of life. If you position yourself to give something back to the world—a message, an inspiration, or an act of service that in some way will leave the world a better place—you're bound to feel less in crisis and more satisfied during this phase of your life.

If you find yourself wondering what's next for you, here are some things to consider:

- Use social media, or the good old-fashioned telephone, to connect with people outside your regular circles to get inspired.
- Find other people doing things that interest you and ask them if you can help.
- Attend a seminar, workshop, or conference. You're sure to find a breakout topic that inspires you.
- Contribute your time, talent, or treasure to a charity that moves you.
- Travel by yourself. Visit a part of the state, country, or world you haven't seen. Time alone in your head, and then in community with people you don't know, will inspire new thoughts and actions.

CARING FOR AGING PARENTS

I recently posted a question on Facebook asking what unique challenges people in their forties face outside of parenting. There were lots of answers from a variety of angles, but "caring for aging parents" was clearly the top lifestyle concern among my peers. Though we're not quite the sandwich generation, at around age forty we do begin caring for our parents at the same time that we must tend to the new and developing needs of our adolescent children. This leaves many of us feeling run down, overcommitted, and stretched thin, so much so that we often give up on taking care of ourselves.

I have watched my friends caring for parents who are suffering from cancer and other serious illnesses, which is both heartbreaking and exhausting for them. But it's not only growing medical needs that demand our attention. Many of our parents don't have adequate retirement savings, so as we're sweating saving for college tuition we may also be wondering how we will supplement our parents' budget, perhaps even housing them, to help them make ends meet.

This phase of life is so hard for me because being a parent puts me at my most vulnerable. Those tender moments of motherliness my mom would provide, from keeping the kids overnight so I could go on a date with my husband to bringing me dinner when I was frazzled, are what kept me from feeling totally alone and helpless many times during my kids' younger years. Now that I am watching her age, I'm not only adding her care to my responsibilities, but I'm losing my helper at the same time. That makes it twice as hard to cope.

Some friendly reminders:

• It's more important than ever to take time for yourself. Find a hobby. Exercise. Eat right. Sleep well. Get outside. Read for pleasure. Be nice to yourself.

• Enlist help. You don't have to do it all. Hire someone to help with parents and with kids. Get neighbors and other family involved. Ask, is there a part of you that needs to control this situation or can you give some of that up?

• Don't make your relationship with your parent all about care. Have fun together. Look at photo albums. Watch movies. Find moments of joy to share.

• Take a look at your parent's future finances now, before it sneaks up on you.

• Start open conversations. "I know it's awkward to talk about money but we don't want to get caught off guard..."

MARRIAGE

When your kids go to middle school, you and your spouse or partner may find yourselves with more time to reconnect, enjoy your favorite activities, and focus lovingly on each other. Or you may find yourselves staring at each other across an empty dinner table, wondering what to talk about.

You've been going at a breakneck speed for more than ten years, keeping up with kids' activities, arranging playdates, volunteering at school, playing games, and answering nonstop questions. Suddenly, it's gotten quiet. Your kids aren't talking to you as much. They're spending more time out of the house or in their rooms. The silence left in their wake can be deafening.

For some couples, switching gears so quickly can be a tough adjustment. I remember when my husband and I were planning our wedding almost twenty years ago, we fantasized about our honeymoon and how we would blissfully kick back with nothing to do but *sit still* and relax. After the hectic pace of the previous few months, though, when the first day of our honeymoon came we hardly knew what to do with ourselves. We fidgeted. We searched for things to talk about now that making lists and finalizing details were done. We didn't seem to know *how* to relax. It was a very odd feeling to have finally reached that glorified landmark and to feel so unexpectedly let down.

This phase of life when your kid heads to middle school can feel the same way. You have been waiting for your kids to be old enough that you didn't have to do everything for them and you could finally have a little time to yourself, and now…huh. It's awfully hard to figure out what to do with yourself, but it's important to make the effort.

DEVOTE TIME TO YOUR MARRIAGE

Like the flight attendants tell you every time you're about to take off, in case of emergency "be sure to adjust your own mask before helping others." This is good advice even before you find yourself in a marital emergency. Making your marriage a priority is ultimately beneficial to your entire family.

- Don't wait a minute longer. Like exercise, the sooner you start, the better you'll feel.
- Figure out what interests you personally, to make life more interesting for both of you. If you're having a hard time finding stuff to talk about maybe you need a hobby.
- Have interesting date nights. Don't just go sit at a restaurant. Go bowling. Take a cooking class. Do CrossFit. Volunteer. Be active.
- Talk about the future. Dare to make a bold plan together for travel or a hobby you both enjoy.

- Talk about the past. Bring out old home movies or photos and get nostalgic.
- Be intimate. Have sex.
- Get counseling if you need help. A professional should be able to get you connecting more quickly than you likely can on your own; the worst tactic is to ignore the growing distance between you and accept it as the new norm.

DIVORCE

Not all problems can be fixed with bowling…or counseling…or the passage of time. For many of you, divorce is slowly and clearly becoming the best choice. I don't, for a second, judge that decision and I know for some of my friends it has meant an exponential growth in happiness for their families.

What you should know about divorce at this stage of life is that it is particularly hard for middle school–aged kids. Divorce is always painful, but research shows that the toughest two times for a kid to go through a parent's divorce are during preschool and middle school.[4] Your middle schooler is struggling with defining his identity, finding acceptance outside of you, and waffling between the world of adults and children. Your divorce will create *more than normal* feelings of insecurity and self-doubt in your kid. We all know that classic line from dating breakups, "It's not you. It's me." If you've been on the receiving end of this one, you probably didn't take that sentiment to heart. Even if you could logically process that the other person's drawbacks were no fault of your own, you probably still had doubts, irrational or not, about what you could have done to save the relationship. The same feelings come up for a child when parents use a similar line of "Our divorce has nothing to do with our love for you. This is about us, not you." Your middle schooler's brain is processing everything from the emotional center. His critical thinking and reasoning skills are on hold. His developing identity project causes him to see everything from an egocentric position. All of this causes him to take your divorce more personally and emotionally than he would at other times.

I'm not saying don't get a divorce while your kid is in middle school. I do believe, however, that if you are in a safe environment, waiting a few years may prove healthier for your child. However, if you decide that it is in everyone's best interest to divorce now, consider these ways to help your child through this time:

- Make consistency and stability the number-one priority for your child right now.
- Create a predictable schedule for coparenting (assuming your ex is a safe parent).
- Make your house feel safe and cozy with predictable routines around meals, bedtime, visitors, etc. Other kids may be toying with more freedom at this age but yours might benefit from a happy, structured environment a little longer.
- Provide a counselor for your child.
- Communicate respectfully and unemotionally with your ex. "Botox Brow" isn't just for teens! It works well here, too.
- Communicate respectfully and appropriately with your tween. Explain things without painting either parent as a villain. It may help to pretend you're explaining the situation to a kid in the neighborhood instead of your own child. Sometimes this can help you sound more reasonable despite your very natural and understandable emotions.
- Worry less about grades. School performance may suffer now.
- Answer questions. Kids in middle school will want to question your decision a lot. They'll also want to challenge you on your choices, in part because that's what kids this age do as they develop hypothetical thinking skills, and in part because they don't like what you're doing and want to change it. Don't deny

your kid the right to ask. Use his questions to get to the root of his fears and address those.

DATING

Being a single parent presents tricky challenges to parents of middle schoolers, but perhaps none as awkward as dating, specifically, dating at a time when your kids are learning more about sex. What they hear on the bus or what they see on TV suddenly becomes, gulp, possibly about you. They may even begin to make judgments about your extracurricular activities ("Gross, you're too old to date."), ask you specifically what you're doing ("Are you two doing it?"), or try to exert some control over your personal decisions, as you do theirs ("You're *not* going out with him!"). These responses may have to do with your kid feeling a loss of control, having a desire to be more grown up, and/or missing a basic measure of impulse control. Remember, even if your kid is out of line, you should still respond by modeling empathy, respect, and maturity.

It's hard to balance your kid's needs with yours when you're a single parent. At times you'll be driven by guilt to compensate for whatever it is you worry she's being deprived of, yet at other times you'll be driven by self-preservation in your need to carve out something personal, something not kid-centric, in your life.

If you're starting to date while your kid is in middle school:

- As much as possible, your tween shouldn't see you dating at all. Since you don't know how she'll react, interpret, or internalize the situation, keep your private life private. This will create a more stable and predictable atmosphere for your child.
- If your dating lifestyle is obvious, model the kind of dating behavior you want your child to eventually assume. Your kid will rationalize risky teen behavior by copying what you do,

not listening to what you say. This means no sleepovers while the kids are at your house.

- Communicate to your kids that they are your priority.
- Have fun! Being restrictive about what your kids experience doesn't mean you can't have fun when they're spending the night at your ex's, their grandparents', or a friend's house.

The bottom line on a lot of these topics is this: you are more than a parent, and you deserve to take time to manage or cultivate other aspects of your life. As your kids grow, they'll look to you as a role model for living a balanced life. Show them that you appreciate your changing body, brain, and identity and they'll learn to give themselves the same grace by your example.

Conclusion

Now that you've had a middle school makeover, I have to say, you look *amazing*.

Just kidding. I mean, you *do* look amazing, but that has nothing to do with me. This makeover was about improving how you feel, not how you look. I hope you feel more confident, relaxed, and enthusiastic about middle school now that you've read this.

You're now the laid-back, confident, nurturing parent of a middle schooler. How many of the following items can you check off with assuredness?

COMPETENCY CHECK FOR PARENTS OF MIDDLE SCHOOLERS

Do you or will you:

- ☐ Encourage your kid to take positive risks?
- ☐ Maintain "Botox Brow" when communicating with your kid?
- ☐ Support positive identity development by allowing freedom of expression through personal choices and individual style?
- ☐ Teach impulse control and critical thinking by being a good assistant manager and not a micromanager?
- ☐ Take your kid's problems seriously, not personally?

☐ Teach your kid to solve her own problems instead of fixing things for her?

☐ Support positive social growth by giving your kid the freedom to make mistakes and learn from them?

☐ Express empathy for your kid's personal problems without passing judgment?

☐ Have a plan for fulfillment, engagement, and satisfaction in your life when your children leave home?

☐ Put yourself first when your batteries need recharging or when you need a change of pace?

Congratulations! Your middle school makeover is complete. If you missed a few, don't worry. Most of these take practice, and lots of it. This is a process and all that matters, really, is that you're making an effort to reach a place of less anxiety and more enthusiasm for the middle school years.

As you go through the next few years, I'll be here if you need me. In the words of Ferris Bueller, "Life moves pretty fast," and though some things about middle school will never change, like the body, brain, and identity issues all kids face, there's a lot of stuff that's going to be hard to keep up with. Just as soon as you've figured out the latest trend or social platform, your kids are on to the next thing. Here are some ways I can help:

My website, MichelleintheMiddle.com, is a resource for parents and teachers. I try to cover the latest trends in my blog to keep you current.

Facebook is where I do most of my talking. Find me there at Facebook.com/middleschoolrelief. Please! I love interacting with parents there.

If you have a specific concern about your child's social experiences in middle school and how you should handle them, I offer coaching packages through Skype.

Leader Guides for my social leadership curriculum, *Athena's Path* (for girls) and *Hero's Pursuit* (for boys) are available for purchase through my website. These will help you organize groups or classes at your school or community organization.

If you have a daughter in rising sixth or seventh grade, you can attend together *Right in the Middle*, a mother–daughter conference I host to prepare you both for middle school.

Finally, I'd love to speak at your next school, organization, or community event.

Thank you for reading this book! You're done. Give yourself a pat on the back and go relax. You deserve it.

Acknowledgments

The staff at Bibliomotion, especially Erika Heilman, who believed in this book and supported my desire to write for a very specific audience, parents of middle schoolers, even when other publishers thought my niche was too small. I am so glad you saw value in talking directly to this important audience.

Quinn Davidson, who defies a title. We have worked together for eight years and you have worn just about every hat a small business requires. You are my PR agent, communications department, administrator, CFO, newspaper reader, cheerleader, devil's advocate, right hand, and friend. Thank you for going on this adventure with me. I would curl up in a ball (much more often) if you weren't right by my side through all of this.

Betsy Thorpe, Dawn O'Malley, and Quinn Davidson, you read this book at varying stages of production from "sh★tty first drafts"[1] to just moments before publishing and offered valuable edits along the way. Rosie Molinary, you gave your endless support of me and of this writing project. Dr. Amy Combs, you contributed your wisdom to the final chapter when I got stuck. I'm grateful to you all.

I don't know how a girl so terrible at making friends in middle school ended up with so many wonderful women in her life. To Sarah Connolly and Jenna Glasser (who came to my rescue in high school and stayed by my side ever since – a lifetime of love!), Jenny O'Brien, Mary Crowe, and Krista Hays (who showed me in college and long after how to step out of my comfort zone and live out loud), Angie Scavone, Kate Weaver, Denise Burkard, Ashley Icard, and Dawn O'Malley (who I met as adults but who can make me laugh like I am thirteen again). You all show me regularly that good friends are wacky, compassionate, kind, and comfortable, and that the best friendships defy both time and geography.

All teachers of Athena's Path and Hero's Pursuit, especially Jen Konstanty, who tells each of her students to remember who they are when they are alone in their room singing into a hairbrush, and to be that person with one another. Special thanks to Jen Boa for proudly carrying the torch with her wherever she goes. Thank you Wes Calbreath for your invaluable "guy perspective" and your inspirational respect for teaching and learning. Thank you Bonnie Kleffman for your years of being a strong role model to girls.

All of the parents I work with (or kill time with on Facebook) who have cheered me toward the finish line of this book. Your enthusiasm was often my fuel.

Ashley Inzer, for your electric creativity and years of unqualified support.

My mother, Sheila, for unconditional love always. For hot meals while I was writing. For unwavering support every step of the way from when I first toddled until today.

My stepfather, Chuck, who raised me and whom I consider my dad. Thank you for putting my education first and making possible this life I love so much.

My children, Ella and Declan, for inspiring me and supporting me along the way, for showing me that the world will be a better place because of your generation, and for being really nice to me when writing made me tired, cranky, and unable to cook. Although I know you secretly loved all the fast food in this house as we approached my deadline.

Most important, my husband, Travis, for making the daily sacrifice of hard work so that our family can live a life of comfort and adventure, and especially so that I can feel free to do this work that brings me such satisfaction and joy. You're the best man I know. I'm glad you talked to me that night at the bar. It turned out really well. I love you.

Endnotes

CHAPTER 1

1. Peter Meyer, "The Middle School Mess," EducationNext, accessed August 1, 2013, http://educationnext.org/the-middle-school-mess/.
2. Steven B. Jackson, "Are the Twos Terrible Everywhere?" *Psychology Today*, November 14, 2011, accessed August 2, 2013, http://www.psychologytoday.com/blog/culture-conscious/201111/are-the-twos-terrible-everywhere.
3. Charisse Nixon, PhD., "Can We Induce Learned Helplessness?" *YouTube*, January 29, 2008, accessed November 12, 2013. http://www.youtube.com/watch?v=p6TONVkJ3eI

CHAPTER 2

1. Leonard Sax, "Gender Differences in the Sequence of Brain Development," Education.com, May 17, 2010, accessed: September 1, 2013, http://www.education.com/reference/article/Ref_Boys_Girls/.

CHAPTER 3

1. Laurence Steinberg, "Risk-Taking In Adolescence: New Perspectives from Brain and Behavioral Science," *Current Directions in Psychological Science* 16 (2007): 55–59.

CHAPTER 4

1. Deborah Yurgelun-Todd, "Emotional and Cognitive Changes During Adolescence," *Current Opinion in Neurobiology* 2, April 17 (2007): 251–57.

PROBLEM #10

1. P. Orpinas, A.M. Horne, X. Song, P.M. Reeves, and H.L. Hsieh, "Dating Trajectories from Middle School to High School: Association with Performance and Drug Use," *Journal of Research on Adolescence* (2013), doi: 10.111/jora.12029.

PROBLEM #11

1. Michael Thompson, *Homesick and Happy* (New York: Random House, 2012), 6.

FINAL THOUGHTS

1. American Society for Aesthetic Plastic Surgery, "Cosmetic Surgery National Data Bank, Statistics 2012," http://www.surgery.org/sites/default/files/ASAPS -2012-Stats.pdf.
2. "Amygdala Responses to Emotionally Valenced Stimuli in Older and Younger Adults," *Psychological Science* (April, 2004), doi: 10.1111/j.0956-7976 .2004.00662.x, vol. 15 no. 4 259–263.
3. Melissa Lee Phillips, "The Mind at Midlife," *American Psychological Association* (April, 2011), http://www.apa.org/monitor/2011/04/mind-midlife.aspx.
4. Judith S. Wallerstein and Sandra Blakeslee, *What About the Kids? Raising Your Children Before, During, and After Divorce* (New York: Hyperion, 2003).

ACKNOWLEDGMENTS

1. Anne Lamott's phrase from *Bird by Bird: Some Instructions on Writing and Life* (New York: Pantheon, 1994).

References

American Society for Aesthetic Plastic Surgery, "Cosmetic Surgery National Data Bank, Statistics 2012," accessed September 12, 2013, http://www.surgery.org/sites/default/files/ASAPS-2012-Stats.pdf.

Jackson, Steven B., "Are the Twos Terrible Everywhere?" *Psychology Today,* November 14, 2011, accessed August 2, 2013, http://www.psychologytoday.com/blog/culture-conscious/201111/are-the-twos-terrible-everywhere.

Mather, Mara; English, T.; Whitfield, S.; Wais, P.; Ochsner, K.; Gabrieli, JD; Carstensen, Laura; *Psychological Science,* "Amygdala Responses to Emotionally Valenced Stimuli in Older and Younger Adults," (April, 2004), accessed September 16, 2013; doi: 10.1111/j.0956-7976.2004.00662.x, vol. 15 no. 4, pp. 259–263.

Meyer, Peter, "The Middle School Mess," EducationNext, accessed August 1, 2013, http://educationnext.org/the-middle-school-mess/.

Nixon, Charisse, PhD. "Can We Induce Learned Helplessness?" *YouTube.* January 29, 2008, accessed November 12, 2013. http://www.youtube.com/watch?v=p6TONVkJ3eI

Orpinas, P., A.M. Horne, X. Song, P.M. Reeves, and H.L. Hsieh, "Dating Trajectories from Middle School to High School: Association with Performance and Drug Use," *Journal of Research on Adolescence* (2013), accessed September 15, 2013, doi: 10.111/jora.12029.

Phillips, Melissa Lee, "The Mind at Midlife," American Psychological Association (April, 2011), accessed September 14, 2013, http://www.apa.org/monitor/2011/04/mind-midlife.aspx

Sax, Leonard, "Gender Differences in the Sequence of Brain Development," Education.com, May 17, 2010, accessed: September 1, 2013, http://www.education.com/reference/article/Ref_Boys_Girls/.

Steinberg, Laurence, "Risk-Taking In Adolescence: New Perspectives from Brain and Behavioral Science," *Current Directions in Psychological Science* 16 (2007): 55–59.

Thompson, Michael, *Homesick and Happy* (New York: Random House, 2012), 6.

Wallerstein, Judith S. and Sandra Blakeslee. *What About the Kids? Raising Your Children Before, During, and After Divorce* (New York: Hyperion, 2004).

Yurgelun-Todd, Deborah, "Emotional and Cognitive Changes During Adolescence," *Current Opinion in Neurobiology* 2, April 17 (2007): 251–57.

Index